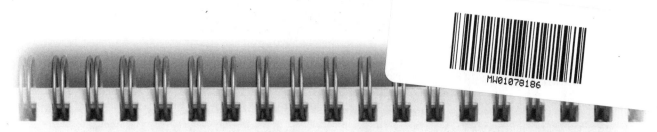

Interactive Notebooks

SCIENCE

Grade 4

Credits

Author: Mary K. Corcoran
Content Editors: Elise Craver, Christine Schwab, Angela Triplett

Visit *carsondellosa.com* for correlations to Common Core, state, national, and Canadian provincial standards.

Carson-Dellosa Publishing, LLC
PO Box 35665
Greensboro, NC 27425 USA
carsondellosa.com

978-1-4838-3124-4
01-341157784

Table of Contents

© Carson-Dellosa • CD-104908

What Are Interactive Notebooks?

Interactive notebooks are a unique form of note taking. Teachers guide students through creating pages of notes on new topics. Instead of being in the traditional linear, handwritten format, notes are colorful and spread across the pages. Notes also often include drawings, diagrams, and 3-D elements to make the material understandable and relevant. Students are encouraged to complete their notebook pages in ways that make sense to them. With this personalization, no two pages are exactly the same.

Because of their creative nature, interactive notebooks allow students to be active participants in their own learning. Teachers can easily differentiate pages to address the levels and needs of each learner. The notebooks are arranged sequentially, and students can create tables of contents as they create pages, making it simple for students to use their notebooks for reference throughout the year. The interactive, easily personalized format makes interactive notebooks ideal for engaging students in learning new concepts.

Using interactive notebooks can take as much or as little time as you like. Students will initially take longer to create pages but will get faster as they become familiar with the process of creating pages. You may choose to only create a notebook page as a class at the beginning of each unit, or you may choose to create a new page for each topic within a unit. You can decide what works best for your students and schedule.

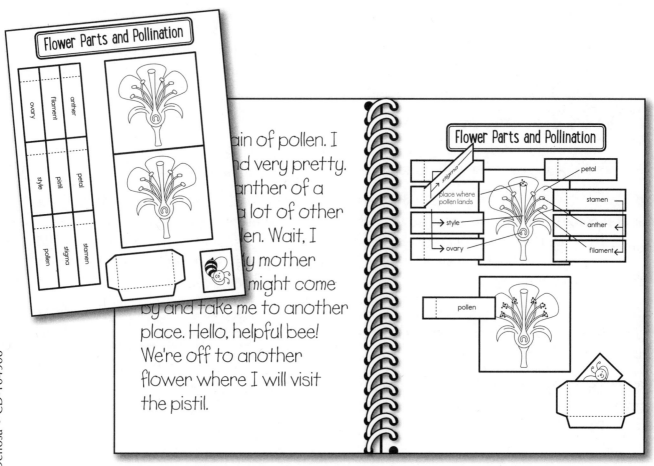

A student's interactive notebook for flower parts and pollination

Getting Started

You can start using interactive notebooks at any point in the school year. Use the following guidelines to help you get started in your classroom. (For more specific details, management ideas, and tips, see page 10.)

1. **Plan each notebook.**

    Use the planning template (page 9) to lay out a general plan for the topics you plan to cover in each notebook for the year.

2. **Choose a notebook type.**

    Interactive notebooks are usually either single-subject, spiral-bound notebooks, composition books, or three-ring binders with loose-leaf paper. Each type presents pros and cons. See page 5 for a more in-depth look at each type of notebook.

3. **Allow students to personalize their notebooks.**

    Have students decorate their notebook covers, as well as add their names and subjects. This provides a sense of ownership and emphasizes the personalized nature of the notebooks.

4. **Number the pages and create the table of contents.**

    Have students number the bottom outside corner of each page, front and back. When completing a new page, adding a table of contents entry will be easy. Have students title the first page of each notebook "Table of Contents." Have them leave several blank pages at the front of each notebook for the table of contents. Refer to your general plan for an idea of about how many entries students will be creating.

5. **Start creating pages.**

    Always begin a new page by adding an entry to the table of contents. Create the first notebook pages along with students to model proper format and expectations.

This book contains individual topics for you to introduce. Use the pages in the order that best fits your curriculum. You may also choose to alter the content presented to better match your school's curriculum. The provided lesson plans often do not instruct students to add color. Students should make their own choices about personalizing the content in ways that make sense to them. Encourage students to highlight and color the pages as they desire while creating them.

After introducing topics, you may choose to add more practice pages. Use the reproducibles (pages 78–96) to easily create new notebook pages for practice or to introduce topics not addressed in this book.

Use the grading rubric (page 11) to grade students' interactive notebooks at various points throughout the year. Provide students copies of the rubric to glue into their notebooks and refer to as they create pages.

What Type of Notebook Should I Use?

Spiral Notebook

The pages in this book are formatted for a standard one-subject notebook.

Pros

- Notebook can be folded in half.
- Page size is larger.
- It is inexpensive.
- It often comes with pockets for storing materials.

Cons

- Pages can easily fall out.
- Spirals can snag or become misshapen.
- Page count and size vary widely.
- It is not as durable as a binder.

Tips

- Encase the spiral in duct tape to make it more durable.
- Keep the notebooks in a central place to prevent them from getting damaged in desks.

Composition Notebook

Pros

- Pages don't easily fall out.
- Page size and page count are standard.
- It is inexpensive.

Cons

- Notebook cannot be folded in half.
- Page size is smaller.
- It is not as durable as a binder.

Tips

- Copy pages meant for standard-sized notebooks at 85 or 90 percent. Test to see which works better for your notebook.

Binder with Loose-Leaf Paper

Pros

- Pages can be easily added, moved, or removed.
- Pages can be removed individually for grading.
- You can add full-page printed handouts.
- It has durable covers.

Cons

- Pages can easily fall out.
- Pages aren't durable.
- It is more expensive than a notebook.
- Students can easily misplace or lose pages.
- Larger size makes it more difficult to store.

Tips

- Provide hole reinforcers for damaged pages.

How to Organize an Interactive Notebook

You may organize an interactive notebook in many different ways. You may choose to organize it by unit and work sequentially through the book. Or, you may choose to create different sections that you will revisit and add to throughout the year. Choose the format that works best for your students and subject.

An interactive notebook includes different types of pages in addition to the pages students create. Non-content pages you may want to add include the following:

Title Page

This page is useful for quickly identifying notebooks. It is especially helpful in classrooms that use multiple interactive notebooks for different subjects. Have students write the subject (such as "Science") on the title page of each interactive notebook. They should also include their full names. You may choose to have them include other information such as the teacher's name, classroom number, or class period.

Table of Contents

The table of contents is an integral part of the interactive notebook. It makes referencing previously created pages quick and easy for students. Make sure that students leave several pages at the beginning of each notebook for a table of contents.

Expectations and Grading Rubric

It is helpful for each student to have a copy of the expectations for creating interactive notebook pages. You may choose to include a list of expectations for parents and students to sign, as well as a grading rubric (page 11).

Unit Title Pages

Consider using a single page at the beginning of each section to separate it. Title the page with the unit name. Add a tab (page 78) to the edge of the page to make it easy to flip to the unit. Add a table of contents for only the pages in that unit.

Glossary

Reserve a six-page section at the back of the notebook where students can create a glossary. Draw a line to split in half the front and back of each page, creating 24 sections. Combine Q and R and Y and Z to fit the entire alphabet. Have students add an entry as each new vocabulary word is introduced.

© Carson-Dellosa • CD-104908

Formatting Student Notebook Pages

The other major consideration for planning an interactive notebook is how to treat the left and right sides of a notebook spread. Interactive journals are usually viewed with the notebook open flat. This creates a left side and a right side. You have several options for how to treat the two sides of the spread.

Traditionally, the right side is used for the teacher-directed part of the lesson, and the left side is used for students to interact with the lesson content. The lessons in this book use this format. However, you may prefer to switch the order for your class so that the teacher-directed learning is on the left and the student input is on the right.

It can also be important to include standards, learning objectives, or essential questions in interactive notebooks. You may choose to write these on the top-left side of each page before completing the teacher-directed page on the right side. You may also choose to have students include the "Introduction" part of each lesson in that same top-left section. This is the *in, through, out* method. Students enter *in* the lesson on the top left of the page, go *through* the lesson on the right page, and exit *out* of the lesson on the bottom left with a reflection activity.

The following chart details different types of items and activities that you could include on each side.

Left Side Student Output	**Right Side** Teacher-Directed Learning
• learning objectives	• vocabulary and definitions
• essential questions	• mini-lessons
• I Can statements	• folding activities
• brainstorming	• steps in a process
• making connections	• example problems
• summarizing	• notes
• making conclusions	• diagrams
• practice problems	• graphic organizers
• opinions	• hints and tips
• questions	• big ideas
• mnemonics	
• drawings and diagrams	

Planning for the Year

Making a general plan for interactive notebooks will help with planning, grading, and testing throughout the year. You do not need to plan every single page, but knowing what topics you will cover and in what order can be helpful in many ways.

Use the Interactive Notebook Plan (page 9) to plan your units and topics and where they should be placed in the notebooks. Remember to include enough pages at the beginning for the non-content pages, such as the title page, table of contents, and grading rubric. You may also want to leave a page at the beginning of each unit to place a mini table of contents for just that section.

In addition, when planning new pages, it can be helpful to sketch the pieces you will need to create. Use the following notebook template and notes to plan new pages.

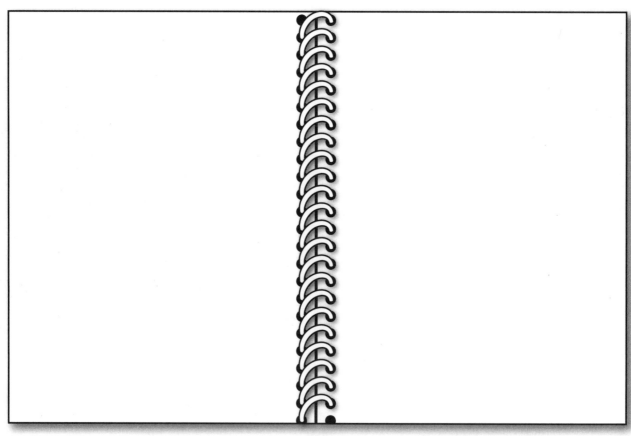

Left Side   **Right Side**

Notes

_____

_____

_____

Interactive Notebook Plan

Page	Topic	Page	Topic
1		51	
2		52	
3		53	
4		54	
5		55	
6		56	
7		57	
8		58	
9		59	
10		60	
11		61	
12		62	
13		63	
14		64	
15		65	
16		66	
17		67	
18		68	
19		69	
20		70	
21		71	
22		72	
23		73	
24		74	
25		75	
26		76	
27		77	
28		78	
29		79	
30		80	
31		81	
32		82	
33		83	
34		84	
35		85	
36		86	
37		87	
38		88	
39		89	
40		90	
41		91	
42		92	
43		93	
44		94	
45		95	
46		96	
47		97	
48		98	
49		99	
50		100	

Managing Interactive Notebooks in the Classroom

Working with Younger Students

- Use your yearly plan to preprogram a table of contents that you can copy and give to students to glue into their notebooks, instead of writing individual entries.

- Have assistants or parent volunteers precut pieces.

- Create glue sponges to make gluing easier. Place large sponges in plastic containers with white glue. The sponges will absorb the glue. Students can wipe the backs of pieces across the sponges to apply the glue with less mess.

Creating Notebook Pages

- For storing loose pieces, add a pocket to the inside back cover. Use the envelope pattern (page 81), an envelope, a jumbo library pocket, or a resealable plastic bag. Or, tape the bottom and side edges of the two last pages of the notebook together to create a large pocket.

- When writing under flaps, have students trace the outline of each flap so that they can visualize the writing boundary.

- Where the dashed line will be hidden on the inside of the fold, have students first fold the piece in the opposite direction so that they can see the dashed line. Then, students should fold the piece back the other way along the same fold line to create the fold in the correct direction.

- To avoid losing pieces, have students keep all of their scraps on their desks until they have finished each page.

- To contain paper scraps and avoid multiple trips to the trash can, provide small groups with small buckets or tubs.

- For students who run out of room, keep full and half sheets available. Students can glue these to the bottom of the pages and fold them up when not in use.

Dealing with Absences

- Create a model notebook for absent students to reference when they return to school.

- Have students cut a second set of pieces as they work on their own pages.

Using the Notebook

- To organize sections of the notebook, provide each student with a sheet of tabs (page 78).

- To easily find the next blank page, either cut off the top-right corner of each page as it is used or attach a long piece of yarn or ribbon to the back cover to be used as a bookmark.

Interactive Notebook Grading Rubric

4

_____ Table of contents is complete.

_____ All notebook pages are included.

_____ All notebook pages are complete.

_____ Notebook pages are neat and organized.

_____ Information is correct.

_____ Pages show personalization, evidence of learning, and original ideas.

3

_____ Table of contents is mostly complete.

_____ One notebook page is missing.

_____ Notebook pages are mostly complete.

_____ Notebook pages are mostly neat and organized.

_____ Information is mostly correct.

_____ Pages show some personalization, evidence of learning, and original ideas.

2

_____ Table of contents is missing a few entries.

_____ A few notebook pages are missing.

_____ A few notebook pages are incomplete.

_____ Notebook pages are somewhat messy and unorganized.

_____ Information has several errors.

_____ Pages show little personalization, evidence of learning, or original ideas.

1

_____ Table of contents is incomplete.

_____ Many notebook pages are missing.

_____ Many notebook pages are incomplete.

_____ Notebook pages are too messy and unorganized to use.

_____ Information is incorrect.

_____ Pages show no personalization, evidence of learning, or original ideas.

Flower Parts and Pollination

Introduction

Divide students into small groups to research and present information on different pollinators such as bees, butterflies, moths, hummingbirds, bats, lizards, and the wind.

Creating the Notebook Page

Guide students through the following steps to complete the right-hand page in their notebooks.

1. Add a Table of Contents entry for the Flower Parts and Pollination pages.

2. Cut out the title and glue it to the top of the page.

3. Cut out one flower and glue it below the title.

4. Cut out all of the flaps except for the *pollen* flap. Apply glue to the back of the left sections and attach the labels to the flower diagram to correctly label the flower. You may need to place the flaps near some parts of the flower and draw connecting lines.

5. Under each flap, describe what the flower part does.

6. Cut out the second flower picture and glue it below the first flower. Draw specks of pollen on all of the anthers in the second picture and the stigma of the first picture.

7. Cut out the *pollen* flap and glue it to the page.

8. Under the flap, describe how pollen moves from one flower to another.

9. Cut out the bee and use it to reenact pollination beside the pollen on the second flower.

10. Cut out the pocket. Apply glue to the back of the tabs and attach it to the bottom corner of the page. It may overlap the bottom flower piece slightly.

11. Store the bee in the pocket created in step 10.

Reflect on Learning

To complete the left-hand page, have students write a short story from the point of view of a grain of pollen. Make sure that students explain the process of pollination from start to finish.

Answer Key

anther: produces pollen; filament: holds up the anther; ovary: location of ovules, it becomes fruit when it ripens; petal: the colorful part of the flower; pistil: the female part of the flower; pollen: made in the anther, used to fertilize an egg to make a seed; stamen: the male part of the flower; stigma: receives the pollen (for example, from an insect or wind); style: holds the stigma

Flower Parts and Pollination

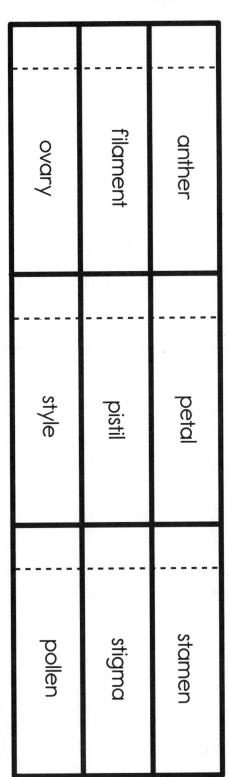

ovary	filament	anther
style	pistil	petal
pollen	stigma	stamen

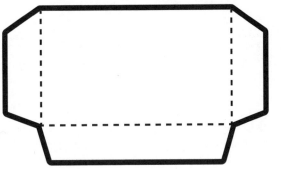

Vertebrates and Invertebrates

Introduction

Distribute pictures of vertebrates and invertebrates to small groups of students. Have them sort them into two groups (vertebrates and invertebrates). Discuss the main difference between these two groups.

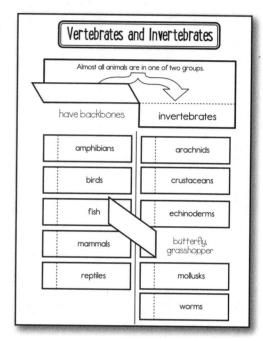

Creating the Notebook Page

Guide students through the following steps to complete the right-hand page in their notebooks.

1. Add a Table of Contents entry for the Vertebrates and Invertebrates pages.

2. Cut out the title and glue it to the top of the page.

3. Cut out the *Almost all animals* flap book. Cut on the solid line to create two flaps. Apply glue to the back of the top section and attach it below the title. Under the flaps, write what defines each category (vertebrates have backbones, invertebrates do not have backbones).

4. Draw a line down the center of the page to divide it in half vertically.

5. Cut out the remaining flaps. Apply glue to the back of the left sections and attach them below the correct category. Under each flap, write several examples of animals that fit in that category.

Reflect on Learning

To complete the left-hand page, write several animals on the board, such as *shark, gorilla, bee, crab,* and *tarantula*. Have students write which group and subcategory each animal belongs in and why.

Answer Key
Examples will vary.
Vertebrates
amphibians: frog, salamander, toad; birds: bluebird, eagle, seagull; fish: puffer fish, sea horse, shark; mammals: elephant, possum, tiger; reptiles: crocodile, snake, turtle
Invertebrates
arachnids: scorpion, spiders, ticks; crustaceans: crayfish, lobster, pill bug; echinoderms: sea cucumber, sea urchin, starfish; insects: butterfly, grasshopper, moth; mollusks: clam, octopus, snail; worms: earthworm, leech, tapeworm

Vertebrates and Invertebrates

Almost all animals are in one of two groups.

vertebrates | invertebrates

amphibians	insects
arachnids	mammals
birds	mollusks
crustaceans	reptiles
echinoderms	worms
fish	

Animal Classification

Introduction

Give each student an object from the classroom, such as a book, pencil, lunch box, etc. Review the definition of classification as an arrangement of objects, ideas, or information into groups where members have one or more characteristics in common. Then, have students choose broad characteristics that describe their items, such as used for writing, green, square, etc. Write six characteristics on the board and try to match each classroom item to a characteristic. Tweak the descriptions as needed.

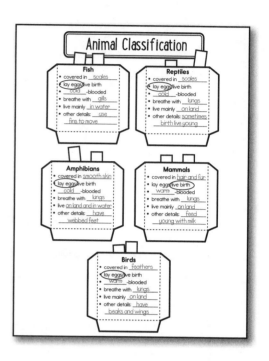

Creating the Notebook Page

Guide students through the following steps to complete the right-hand page in their notebooks.

1. Add a Table of Contents entry for the Animal Classification pages.

2. Cut out the title and glue it to the top of the page.

3. Cut out the five animal classification pockets. Apply glue to the back of the tabs and attach them to the page.

4. Fill in the blanks on each pocket with the correct information. For the lay *eggs/live birth* line, circle the correct characteristic.

5. Cut out the word strips. Sort the animals into the correct pockets. (Cut up index cards to add more animals if desired.)

Reflect on Learning

To complete the left-hand page, have students create a new animal species. They should draw a picture of their animal, describe its physical and behavioral characteristics, describe its habitat, and create a name for it. Then, students should explain how their animal would be classified and why.

Answer Key
Fish: covered in scales, lay eggs, cold-blooded, breathe with gills, live mainly in water, another detail may include: there are both freshwater and saltwater species, (tuna, shark); Reptiles: covered in scales, lay eggs, cold-blooded, breathe with lungs, live mainly on land, another detail may include: some reptiles, such as snakes, can live on land or in the water, (lizard, crocodile); Amphibians: covered in smooth, moist skin, lay eggs, cold-blooded, breathe with lungs, live mainly on land, another detail may include: they often have webbed feet, (frog, salamander); Mammals: covered in hair or fur, live birth, warm-blooded, breathe with lungs, live mainly on land, another detail may include: mammals feed milk to their young, (dolphin, bear); Birds: covered in feathers, lay eggs, warm-blooded, breathe with lungs, live mainly in trees, another detail may include: birds have beaks and wings, (flamingo, penguin)

Animal Classification

Fish
- covered in ___________
- lay eggs/live birth
- _________-blooded
- breathe with __________
- live mainly ___________
- other details: __________

  ____

Reptiles
- covered in ___________
- lay eggs/live birth
- _________-blooded
- breathe with __________
- live mainly ___________
- other details: __________

  ____

Amphibians
- covered in ___________
- lay eggs/live birth
- _________-blooded
- breathe with __________
- live ________________
- other details: __________

  ____

Mammals
- covered in ___________
- lay eggs/live birth
- _________-blooded
- breathe with __________
- live mainly ___________
- other details: __________

  ____

Birds
- covered in ___________
- lay eggs/live birth
- _________-blooded
- breathe with __________
- live mainly ___________
- other details: __________

  ____

bear	crocodile	dolphin	flamingo	frog	lizard	penguin	salamander	shark	tuna

Getting Energy

Each student will need a brass paper fastener to complete this page.

Introduction

Ask students about their favorite restaurants and what they like to eat there. Divide students into small groups to list the people and places involved in getting their favorite foods to their plates. Compare and contrast this process to how wild animals get food.

Creating the Notebook Page

Guide students through the following steps to complete the right-hand page in their notebooks.

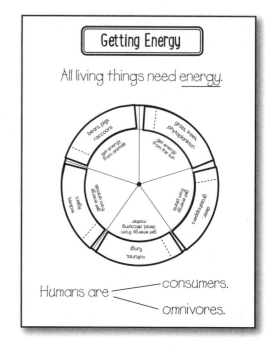

1. Add a Table of Contents entry for the Getting Energy pages.

2. Cut out the title and glue it to the top of the page.

3. Below the title, write a statement describing the relationship between organisms and energy.

4. Cut out both circles. Place the smallest circle on the bottom with the gray side down. Push a brass paper fastener through the center dots to connect the circles. It may be helpful to create the hole in each piece separately first. Apply glue to the gray glue section of the small circle and glue the piece below the title. The circle should spin freely. Do not press the brass paper fastener through the page.

5. Cut out the five flaps. Apply glue to the back of the left sections and attach them in the blank spaces around the outside of the circle, matching each flap to the correct description in the center of the circle.

6. Under each flap, write whether the organisms are *producers, consumers,* or *decomposers.* For the consumers, you may want to specify if they are herbivores, carnivores, or omnivores.

7. On the bottom of the page, describe how humans get energy and what category they fit in.

Reflect on Learning

To complete the left-hand page, have students give an example of each term: *producer, consumer, herbivore, carnivore, omnivore,* and *decomposer.*

Getting Energy

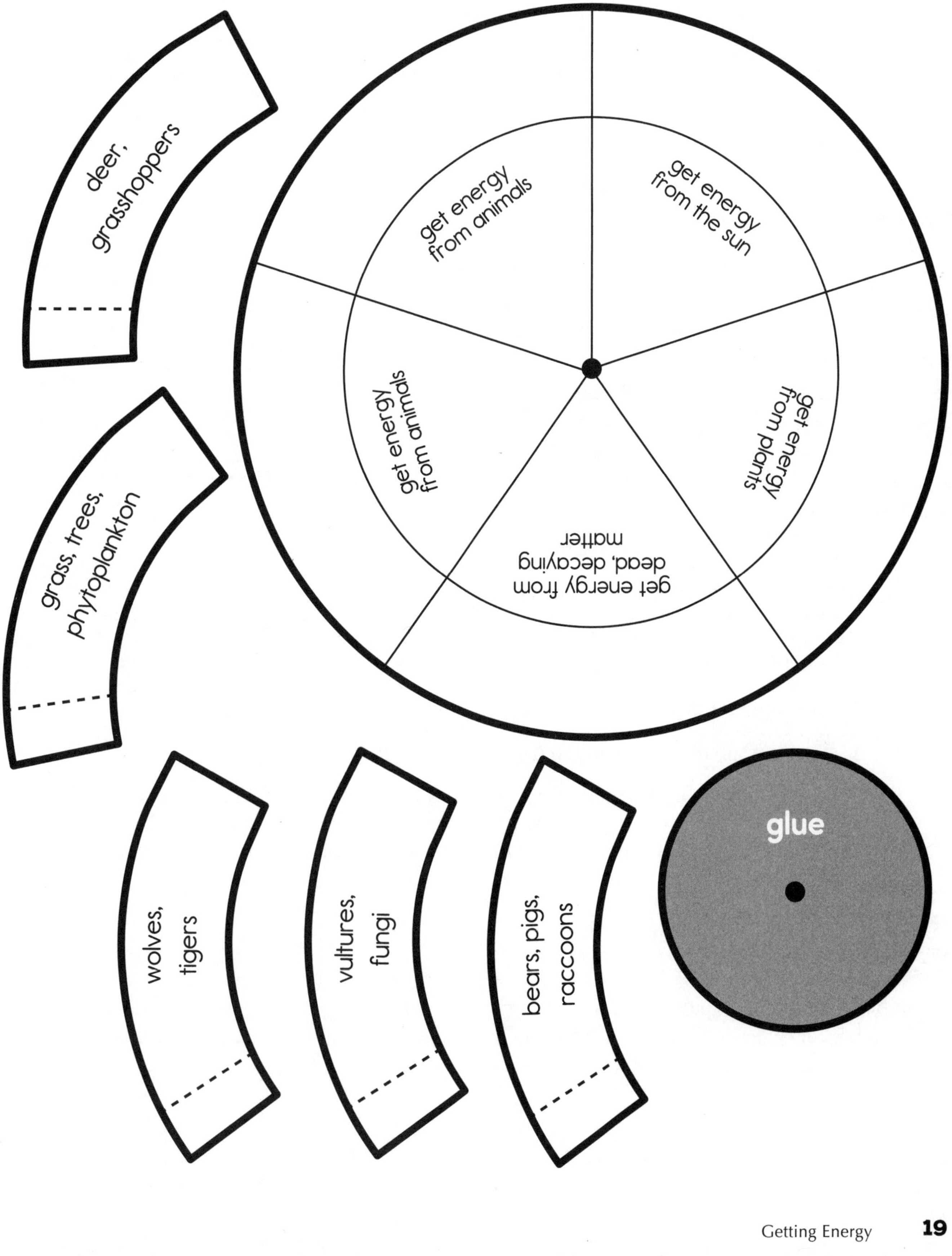

get energy
from animals

get energy
from the sun

get energy
from animals

get energy
from plants

get energy from
dead, decaying
matter

deer,
grasshoppers

grass, trees,
phytoplankton

wolves,
tigers

vultures,
fungi

bears, pigs,
raccoons

glue

Food Chains and Webs

Introduction

Discuss how all living things get energy from food. Green plants use energy from the sun to make their food. Plants use the food they make for energy to grow. Animals get energy by eating plants or other animals. Give students several strips of construction paper. Have them write the name of an animal and draw the animal on the first strip of paper. Then, each student should continue making a chain with the paper strips to demonstrate his animal's food chain. For example, if students draw a hawk on the first strip, they may draw a snake on the second strip, a bug on the third strip, grass on the fourth strip, and a sun on the last strip to complete the chain. Students should hook the chains together in the correct order to form their food chains.

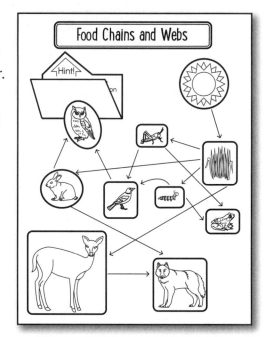

Creating the Notebook Page

Guide students through the following steps to complete the right-hand page in their notebooks.

1. Add a Table of Contents entry for the Food Chains and Webs pages.

2. Cut out the title and glue it to the top of the page.

3. Cut out the *Hint* piece. Fold in on the dashed line. Apply glue to the back of the top half and attach it near the top of the page.

4. Discuss the energy flow of a food web or chain.

5. Cut out the sun and glue it to the page beside the *Hint* piece.

6. Cut out the plants and animals. Choose several of them that would make a complete food chain. Glue them in order and draw arrows between them to show the food chain. Then, continue adding plants and animals to create a food web. Draw arrows to show the energy flow through the web. You may not use all of the pieces.

Reflect on Learning

To complete the left-hand page, have students choose another ecosystem (forest, wetland, tundra, etc.) and make a food chain or food web using some of the plants and animals from that ecosystem. Students should use arrows to indicate the flow of energy.

Food Chains and Webs

Hint!

In a food chain or a food web, the direction of the arrow always shows the direction that the energy flows.

- - - - - - - - - - - -

 energy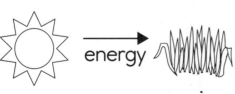

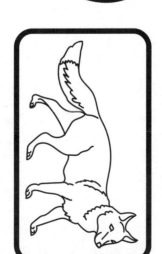

Traits and Heredity

Introduction

Provide students with pictures of baby or adult animals. Each adult animal should match a baby animal. Have students walk around to find pictures of the adults or babies that match their pictures. Students should explain how they knew they had found the correct match. As a class, discuss how inherited features are passed down from parents to children. Discuss how learned behaviors change as animals interact with their environment. Some behaviors, like returning to a nesting site, are instinctive. Learned behaviors are taught or caused by experiences.

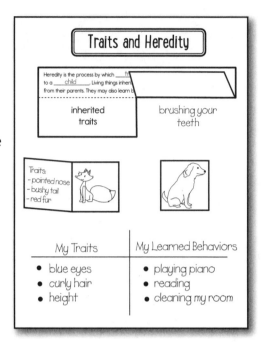

Creating the Notebook Page

Guide students through the following steps to complete the right-hand page in their notebooks.

1. Add a Table of Contents entry for the Traits and Heredity pages.

2. Cut out the title and glue it to the top of the page.

3. Cut out the *Heredity is* piece. Cut on the solid line to create two flaps. Apply glue to the back of the top section and attach it below the title.

4. Complete the explanation. (Heredity is the process by which **characteristics** are passed from **parents** to a **child**. Living things inherit **traits**, or physical characteristics, from their parents. They may also learn behaviors from them.) Under each flap, write an example of a trait or an example of a learned behavior.

5. Cut out the fox and dog T-shaped pieces. Fold the flaps on the dashed lines so that the blank flaps are under the flaps with the art. Apply glue to the gray glue sections and attach them to the center of the page.

6. Cut out the fox kit and puppy pieces. Glue each piece to the correct inside, blank flap. Discuss the similar, inherited traits between the parents and their children.

7. Write traits and learned behaviors for each animal on the back of the top flaps.

8. On the bottom of the page, make a T-chart. Label it *My Traits* and *My Learned Behaviors*. Complete the chart with your own traits and behaviors.

Reflect on Learning

To complete the left-hand page, have students respond to the following prompts: *How is a learned behavior in an animal different from a behavior that the animal is born with? How can you distinguish between a learned behavior and an instinctive behavior?*

22

Heredity is the process by which _____ are passed from _____ to a _____. Living things inherit _____, or physical characteristics, from their parents. They may also learn behaviors from them.

inherited traits	learned behaviors

Traits and Heredity

Adaptations

Introduction

Display a picture of an arctic fox and a desert fox. Have students compare and contrast the different animals. (For example, the desert fox has large ears and short fur, whereas the arctic fox has small ears and thick, insulating fur.) Make a list of each adaptation on the board. For each adaptation, have students try to give a reason why it helps the fox survive in its environment. Explain that foxes that live in snowy environments have different adaptations from foxes that live in a desert because they need different things in order to survive in their environments.

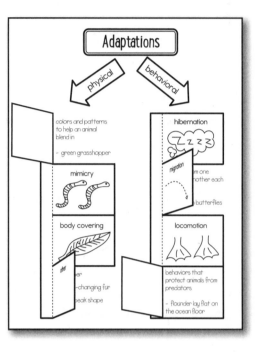

Creating the Notebook Page

Guide students through the following steps to complete the right-hand page in their notebooks.

1. Add a Table of Contents entry for the Adaptations pages.

2. Cut out the title and glue it to the top of the page.

3. Cut out the two arrows and glue them below the title so that they are each pointing downward at an angle.

4. Cut out the two flap books. Cut on the solid lines to create four flaps on each book. Decide which flap book contains physical adaptations and which flap book contains behavioral adaptations. Apply glue to the back of the left sections and attach them to the page below the correct arrows.

5. Discuss the difference between physical and behavioral adaptations. On the front of each flap, draw an example or a representation of the adaptation. Under each flap, define the adaptation and give an example.

Reflect on Learning

To complete the left-hand page, have each student choose a plant or animal from two different environments, such as a cactus and a fern or a polar bear and a black bear. Then, have them compare and contrast the two plants or animals and their adaptations using vocabulary from the right-hand page.

Adaptations

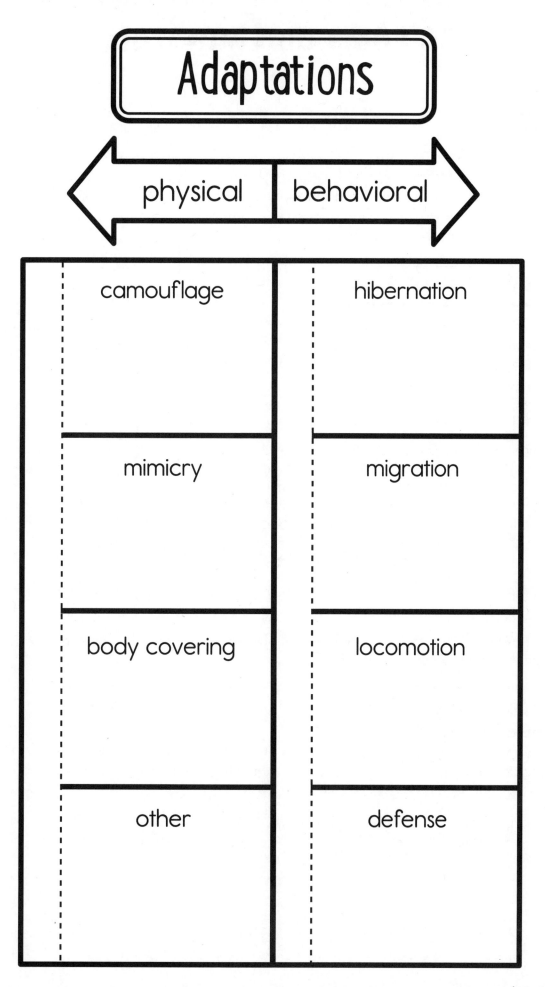

physical	behavioral
camouflage	hibernation
mimicry	migration
body covering	locomotion
other	defense

Vitamins and Minerals

Introduction

Have students guess, "What am I?" Give clues such as, *I am a liquid, I have been pasteurized,* and *I provide calcium.* Share the answer (milk). Discuss how different foods provide different vitamins and minerals. Have students name some vitamins and minerals that they are familiar with and what foods provide them.

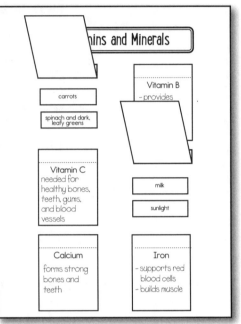

Creating the Notebook Page

Guide students through the following steps to complete the right-hand page in their notebooks.

1. Add a Table of Contents entry for the Vitamins and Minerals pages.

2. Cut out the title and glue it to the top of the page.

3. Cut out the flaps. Apply glue to the back of the top sections and attach them to the page. List the functions (jobs) of each vitamin or mineral on each flap. (Vitamin A: promotes healthy immune systems, healthy skin and eyes, and growth and development; Vitamin B: provides energy and supports body functions; Vitamin C: needed for healthy bones, teeth, gums, and blood vessels; Vitamin D: strengthens bones and teeth; Calcium: forms strong bones and teeth; Iron: supports red blood cells, builds muscle)

4. Cut out the food pieces. Glue each food piece to the page under the vitamin or mineral it supplies the most of.

5. Discuss how some foods may fit in several places because a single food can provide many vitamins and minerals.

Reflect on Learning

To complete the left-hand page, have students design one-day healthy meal plans for their families, taking into consideration any food allergies. Students should explain their food choices.

Answer Key
Answers will vary but may include: Vitamin A: carrots, spinach and dark, leafy greens, eggs, milk; Vitamin B: beans, chicken, eggs, fish, red meat and turkey; Vitamin C: broccoli, green vegetables, tomatoes, and strawberries; Vitamin D: milk, sunlight; Calcium: broccoli, cheese, milk, and yogurt; Iron: beans, chicken, spinach and dark, leafy greens, fish, pumpkin seeds, red meat and turkey

Vitamins and Minerals

beans	broccoli	carrots	cheese
chicken	eggs	fish	green vegetables
milk	red meat and turkey	pumpkin seeds	spinach and dark, leafy greens
strawberries	sunlight	tomatoes	yogurt

Vitamin A	Vitamin B
Vitamin C	Vitamin D
Calcium	Iron

Matter

Introduction

Before the lesson, write names of objects and other words on index cards. Include a mix of concrete items, such as *cup*, *apple*, *pencil*, *air*, and *balloon*, and non-tangible items, such as *sound*, *jumping*, *thoughts*, *shadows*, and *today's date*. Give each student a card. Create a T-chart on the board and label the sides *Matter* and *Not Matter*. As a class, discuss that matter is anything that has mass and takes up space. Have students sort their cards into the correct categories on the board, pausing as necessary to clear up any misconceptions.

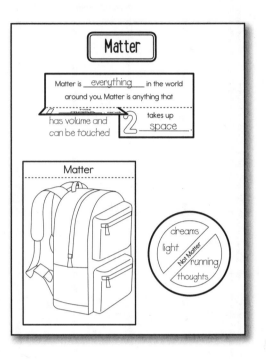

Creating the Notebook Page

Guide students through the following steps to complete the right-hand page in their notebooks.

1. Add a Table of Contents entry for the Matter pages.

2. Cut out the title and glue it to the top of the page.

3. Cut out the *Matter is* flap book. Cut on the solid line to create two flaps. Apply glue to the back of the top section and attach it to the page below the title.

4. Complete the explanation. (Matter is **everything** in the world around you. Matter is anything that 1) has **mass**, and 2) takes up **space**.) Under each flap, explain what it means to have mass and take up space.

5. Cut out the backpack flap. Apply glue to the back of the top section and glue it to the bottom left side of the page.

6. Cut out the six objects.

7. Glue the objects under the backpack flap. Discuss how each of the items are examples of matter, including the backpack itself.

8. Cut out the *Not matter* circle and glue it to the right of the backpack.

9. Write examples of things that are not matter on the circle, such as *ideas*, *light*, and *shadows*.

Reflect on Learning

To complete the left-hand page, have students work in groups to answer the question: *Can you ever destroy matter?* (Hint: Burning does not destroy matter, but it changes it.)

Matter

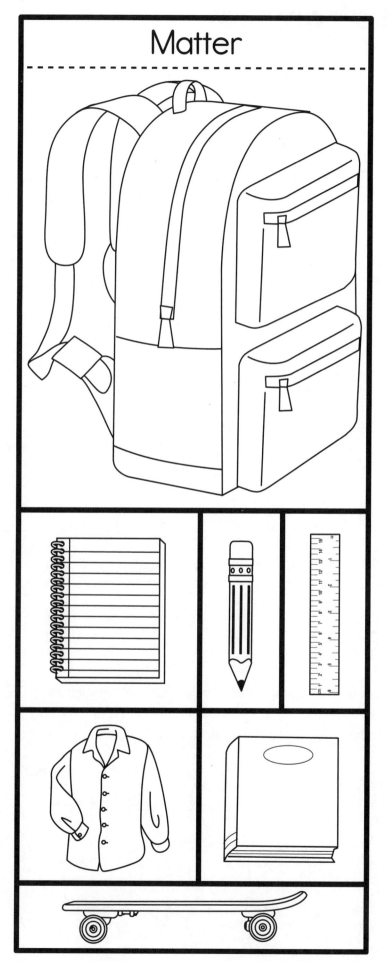

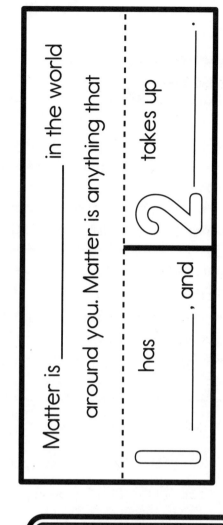

Matter is _____ in the world around you. Matter is anything that

2 takes up

1 has _____, and _____.

Matter

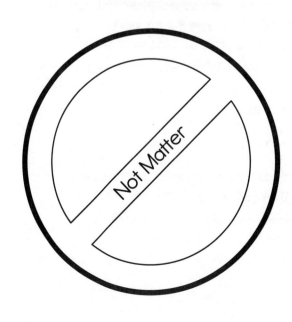

Not Matter

States of Matter

Introduction

Review solids, liquids, and gases. Have students work in small groups to list the solids, liquids, and gases in the classroom. Have each group share their lists. Award each group a point for every unique item on their lists.

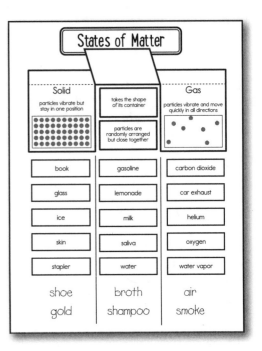

Creating the Notebook Page

Guide students through the following steps to complete the right-hand page in their notebooks.

1. Add a Table of Contents entry for the States of Matter pages.

2. Cut out the title and glue it to the top of the page.

3. Cut out the *Solid, Liquid, Gas* flap book. Cut on the solid lines to create three flaps. Apply glue the back of the top section and attach it below the title.

4. On each flap, draw the way particles look for each state of matter in the box provided.

5. Cut out the six description pieces.

6. Read each description and glue it to the page under the correct flap.

7. Cut out the examples. Draw vertical lines between and below the flaps to divide the page into three columns. Glue each example to the page below the correct state of matter. Write two more examples under each list.

Reflect on Learning

To complete the left-hand page, have students write a paragraph describing a short part of their day, making sure to include as many of the solids, liquids, and gases they interact with in that time period as possible. Then, have students circle each solid in blue, each liquid in yellow, and each gas in orange.

Answer Key
Solid: particles are close and arranged in a pattern, has a fixed shape; book, glass, ice, skin, stapler; Liquid: particles are randomly arranged but close together, takes the shape of its container; gasoline, lemonade, milk, saliva, water; Gas: particles are randomly arranged and far apart, will completely fill its container; car exhaust, carbon dioxide, helium, oxygen, water vapor

States of Matter

Solid	Liquid	Gas
particles vibrate but stay in one position	particles vibrate and move around	particles vibrate and move quickly in all directions

particles are close and arranged in a pattern	particles are randomly arranged but close together	particles are randomly arranged and far apart
has a fixed shape	takes the shape of its container	will completely fill its container

book	car exhaust	carbon dioxide
gasoline	glass	helium
ice	lemonade	milk
oxygen	saliva	skin
stapler	water	water vapor

Temperature and Water

Introduction

Have students guess the highest air temperature ever recorded on Earth (Death Valley, California, 1913; 134°F). Next, have students guess the lowest air temperature ever recorded on Earth (Antarctica, 1983; -89°F). Review the freezing, melting, boiling, and condensation points of water.

Creating the Notebook Page

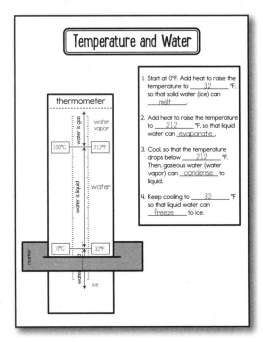

Guide students through the following steps to complete the right-hand page in their notebooks.

1. Add a Table of Contents entry for the Temperature and Water pages.

2. Cut out the title and glue it to the top of the page.

3. Cut out the *thermometer* flap. Apply glue to the back of the top section and attach it to the left side of the page.

4. Label the freezing point/melting point (**0°C**; **32°F**) and the boiling point/condensation point (**100°C**; **212°F**) on the thermometer. Label the thermometer with the names of each state of matter for water (*water is solid: **ice**, water is liquid: **water**,* and *water is gas: **water vapor***). If desired, shade each section a different color.

5. Color the *marker* piece any color and cut it out. Fold on the dashed line to make it easier to cut on the solid line. Insert the opening of the marker over the bottom of the thermometer to serve as a way to raise or lower the temperature of the thermometer (for use with the numbered piece). Apply glue to the bottom of the thermometer flap and attach it to the page to secure the marker in place.

6. Cut out the numbered piece and glue it to the right side of the page.

7. Complete the numbered piece. (1. Start at 0°F. Add heat to raise the temperature to **32**°F so that solid water (ice) can **melt**. 2. Add heat to raise the temperature to **212**°F so that liquid water can **evaporate**. 3. Cool, so that the temperature drops below **212**°F. Then, gaseous water (water vapor) can **condense** to liquid. 4. Keep cooling to **32**°F, so that liquid water can **freeze** to ice.) Discuss what happens to the water at each point.

Reflect on Learning

To complete the left-hand page, have students use what they know about how particles behave for each state of matter to draw a diagram. The diagram should show each state change for water and how the particles are affected as the temperature changes.

Temperature and Water

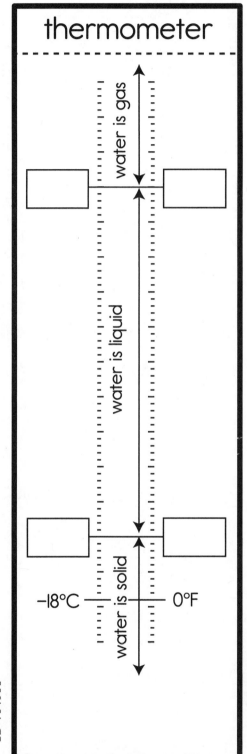

thermometer

water is gas

water is liquid

water is solid

−18°C   0°F

1. Start at 0°F. Add heat to raise the temperature to _____ °F, so that solid water (ice) can _____.

2. Add heat to raise the temperature to _____ °F, so that liquid water can _____.

3. Cool, so that the temperature drops below _____ °F. Then, gaseous water (water vapor) can _____ to liquid.

4. Keep cooling to _____ °F so that liquid water can _____ to ice.

marker

Mass and Weight

Introduction

Have students discuss ways that their backpacks could be lighter without taking anything out. Review the meaning of gravity.

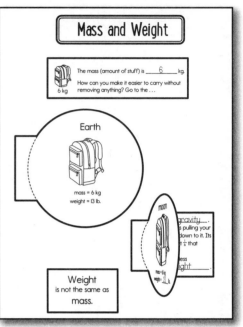

Creating the Notebook Page

Guide students through the following steps to complete the right-hand page in their notebooks.

1. Add a Table of Contents entry for the Mass and Weight pages.

2. Cut out the title and glue it to the top of the page.

3. Cut out *The mass (amount of stuff)* piece and glue it below the title. Complete the sentence. (The mass (amount of stuff) is **6** kg.) Read the question and discuss possible answers.

4. Cut out the *Earth* flap. Apply glue to the back of the left section and attach it below the *The mass (amount of stuff)* piece. Discuss how the mass of the backpack is 6 kilograms, but the weight is 13 pounds.

5. Cut out the *Because of* piece and glue it under the *Earth* flap. Complete the explanation. (Because of **gravity**, Earth is pulling your backpack down to it. Its pull is **13** pounds, which is its **weight**.)

6. Cut out the *moon* flap. Apply glue to the back of the left section and attach it to the bottom right side of the page.

7. Cut out the *Due to* piece and glue it under the *moon* flap. Complete the explanation. (Due to **gravity**, the moon is pulling your backpack down to it. Its pull is about ⅙ that of Earth's. Less pull = less **weight**.)

8. Write the weight on the backpack on the front of the *moon* flap (2.16 lb). Discuss how gravity affects weight but not mass

9. Cut out the *Weight is not the same as* piece and glue it to the bottom left side of the page. Discuss how weight and mass are similar and different.

Reflect on Learning

To complete the left-hand page, have students draw a comic strip showing themselves as astronauts traveling to the moon and back to Earth. In their comic strips, students should show the difference between weight and mass.

Mass and Weight

The mass (amount of stuff) is _____ kg.

How can you make it easier to carry without removing anything? Go to the . . .

6 kg

Weight
is not the same as **mass.**

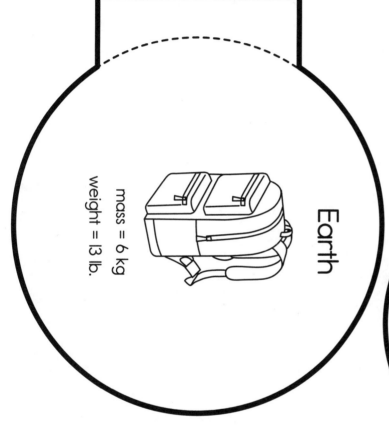

Earth

mass = 6 kg
weight = 13 lb.

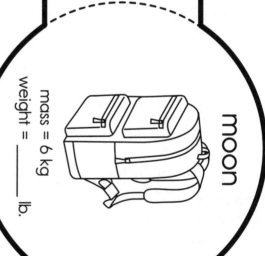

moon

mass = 6 kg
weight = _____ lb.

Because of _____ , Earth is pulling your backpack down to it. Its pull is _____ pounds, which is its _____ .

Due to _____ , the moon is pulling your backpack down to it. Its pull is about $\frac{1}{6}$ that of Earth's.
Less pull = less _____ .

Mixtures

Introduction

Have students "make" a mixture. Draw a large bowl on the board. Have students add different components to it, such as lettuce, spinach, chopped tomatoes, sliced cucumbers, olives, cheese, etc., by drawing them in the bowl. Have students discuss why this salad is a mixture. Have a student remove an ingredient by erasing it. Discuss how mixtures can be separated back into their individual components.

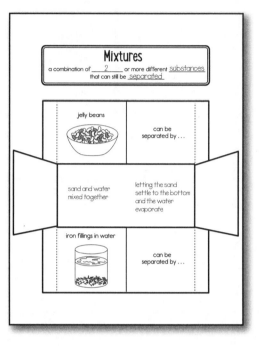

Creating the Notebook Page

Guide students through the following steps to complete the right-hand page in their notebooks.

1. Add a Table of Contents entry for the Mixtures pages.

2. Cut out the title and glue it to the top of the page.

3. Complete the definition (a combination of **two** or more different **substances** that can still be **separated**).

4. Cut out the flap book. Cut along the center line to separate it into two three-flap flap books. Cut on the solid lines to create three flaps on each. Apply glue to the back of the left and right sections and attach them to the page so that the flaps meet in the center.

5. On each flap, draw or color to show the mixture in the container. Under the left flap, describe how it is a true mixture. Under the right flap, describe how you would separate the different substances in the mixture.

Reflect on Learning

To complete the left-hand page, have students describe two mixtures they might find at a party. They should also describe how they would separate each mixture.

Mixtures

a combination of _____ or more different _____
that can still be _____

jelly beans 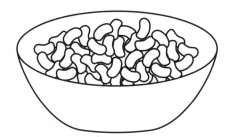	can be separated by . . .
sandy water 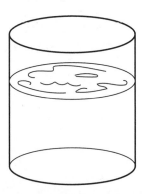	can be separated by . . .
iron fillings in water 	can be separated by . . .

Solutions

Introduction

Fill two large beakers (or other clear jars) with water. Add sugar or salt to one and sand or soil to the other. Observe and compare what happens to the mixture in each jar. Discuss how the sugar disappeared, or *dissolved* (the sugar or salt became a part of the water), into the water, while the sand did not dissolve. Explain that both jars contain a mixture, but the sugar jar contains a *solution*.

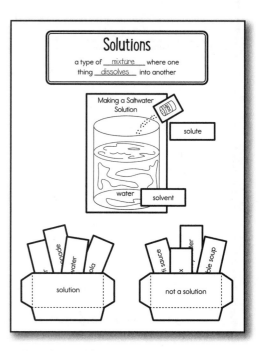

Creating the Notebook Page

Guide students through the following steps to complete the right-hand page in their notebooks.

1. Add a Table of Contents entry for the Solutions pages.

2. Cut out the title and glue it to the top of the page.

3. Complete the definition of solution (a type of **mixture** where one thing **dissolves** into another).

4. Cut out the *Making a Saltwater Solution* piece and glue it below the title.

5. Cut out the *salt, solute,* and *solvent* pieces. Glue the salt above the cup to show salt being added. Draw salt crystals being poured into the water. Glue *solute* near the salt to label it. Glue *solvent* near the water to label it.

6. Cut out the pockets. Apply glue to the back of the tabs and attach them to the bottom of the page.

7. Cut out the example pieces.

8. Read each example. Place it in the correct pocket.

Reflect on Learning

To complete the left-hand page, have students create a graphic organizer to explain the relationship between mixtures and solutions. Have students include examples as part of their graphic organizers.

Answer Key
Solution: air, cola, lemonade, saltwater; Not a solution: sandy water, spaghetti sauce, trail mix, vegetable soup

Solutions

a type of _____ where one

thing _____ into another

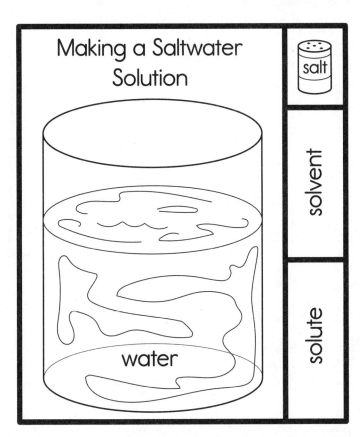

Making a Saltwater Solution

salt

solvent

solute

water

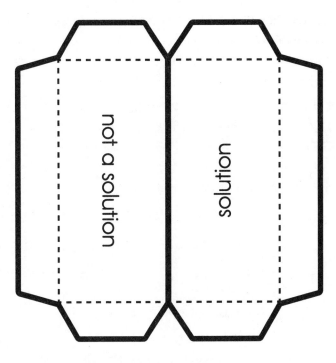

not a solution

solution

air	sandy water
cola	spaghetti sauce
lemonade	trail mix
saltwater	vegetable soup

Types of Energy

Introduction

Draw a concept map on the board with the word *energy* in the center. Ask students what comes to mind when they hear the word *energy.* Write students' responses on the board. Discuss the five forms of energy and give an example of each form. Have students match their earlier responses on the board to an energy type where possible. Next, hold a ball in your hand. Explain how this is potential energy (stored positional energy). Drop the ball and explain that this is kinetic energy (energy of motion). Have students hold a small object, such as a pencil or an eraser. Then, have them use the item to correctly demonstrate the terms as you say "potential" and "kinetic" aloud.

Creating the Notebook Page

Guide students through the following steps to complete the right-hand page in their notebooks.

1. Add a Table of Contents entry for the Types of Energy pages.

2. Cut out the title and glue it to the top of the page.

3. Cut out the two flap books. Cut on the solid lines to create a trifold with three flaps and a trifold with two flaps. Fold the flaps in on the dashed line. Then, fold the bottom flaps up on the dashed line to create trifolds. Apply glue to the gray glue sections and attach them below the title.

4. On the front of each flap, draw an example of the given energy type. Under each flap, describe the energy type.

5. Cut out the flap book with pictures. Apply glue to the back of the center section and attach it to the bottom of the page.

6. Look at each picture and label the type of energy described (**potential** or **kinetic**). Define each type of energy under the flaps.

Reflect on Learning

To complete the left-hand page, have each student design an amusement park. The amusement park should feature five games or attractions that incorporate each of the five types of energy. Students should explain how each attraction or game incorporates a type of energy.

Types of Energy

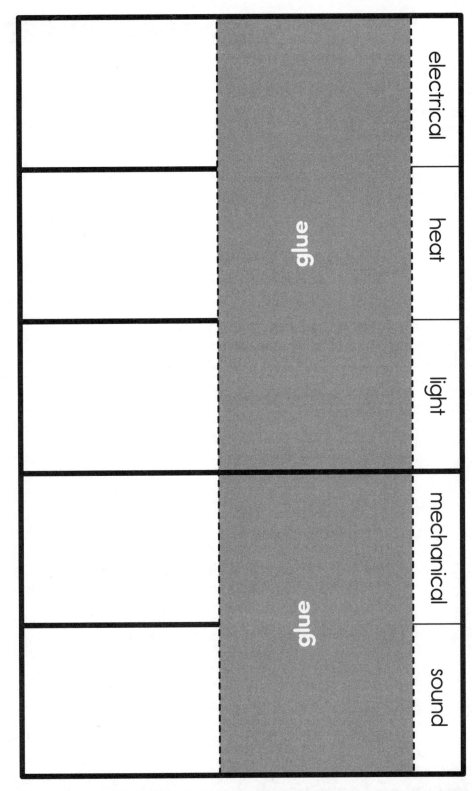

electrical	heat	light	mechanical	sound

glue

glue

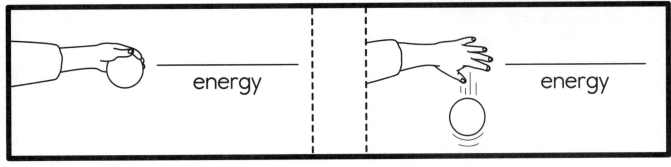

_____ energy

_____ energy

Changes in Energy

Each student will need two brass paper fasteners to complete this page.

Introduction

Discuss the definition of energy as the ability to do work, to make things happen, and to cause changes. Explain that energy cannot be made or destroyed; it can only be changed into different forms. Have students rub their hands together. Ask them what type of energy they are demonstrating (mechanical). Then, ask them if they notice a by-product of the rubbing (heat). They have observed one type of energy being changed to another type.

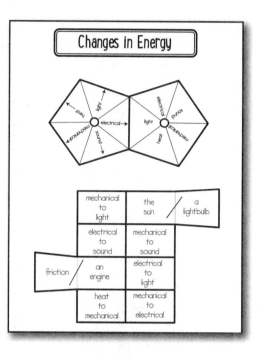

Creating the Notebook Page

Guide students through the following steps to complete the right-hand page in their notebooks.

1. Add a Table of Contents entry for the Changes in Energy pages.

2. Cut out the title and glue it to the top of the page.

3. Cut out the two pentagons and two circles. Place each pentagon on top of a circle with the gray side down. Push a brass paper fastener through the dots to attach the circles. It may be helpful to create the hole in each piece separately first. Apply glue to the gray glue section of each small circle and attach them side by side below the title so that the pentagon with the arrows is on the left. The circles should spin freely. Do not press the brass paper fasteners through the page.

4. Cut out the shutter fold. Cut on the solid lines to create four flaps on each side. Fold the flaps in on the dashed lines over the blank side. Apply glue to the gray glue section and attach it to the bottom of the page.

5. Spin each spinner to create a match. Record the match on a flap. Under the flap, write one or more examples of the energy changes. (Note: Mechanical to sound is not the same as sound to mechanical, and there are not enough flaps for all matches can be recorded.)

Reflect on Learning

To complete the left-hand page, have students think of one object, such as a lightbulb, that changes energy forms. Students should draw diagrams showing the energy change of their objects and label the different forms of changing energy.

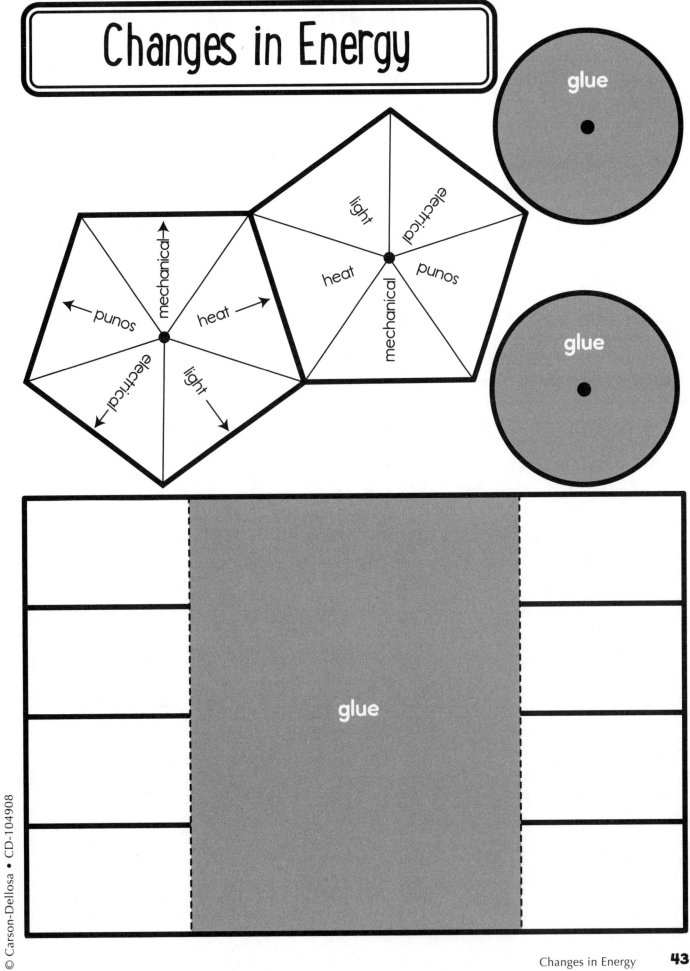

Changes in Energy

glue

glue

glue

Light

Introduction

Review how light can be reflected, refracted, or absorbed by matter. Refraction occurs when light bends as it travels through a substance such as a glass or water. Reflection occurs when light bounces off of things. Light that hits a surface but is not reflected or refracted is absorbed. Absorption causes light to transform into another type of energy, usually thermal energy. Provide students with three different colors of self-stick notes. Challenge them to stick one color on a reflective classroom surface, a second color on a refractive classroom surface, and the last color on an absorbent surface. Review students' choices and discuss any misconceptions.

Creating the Notebook Page

Guide students through the following steps to complete the right-hand page in their notebooks.

1. Add a Table of Contents entry for the Light pages.

2. Cut out the title and glue it to the top of the page.

3. Cut out the *Light is a form of* piece and glue it below the title.

4. Complete the definition of light. (Light is a form of **energy** that travels in a **straight line**. It can be **reflected**, **refracted**, or **absorbed**.)

5. Cut out the three flaps. Apply glue to the back of the top section of each and attach them in a V-formation to the page.

6. Draw lines from the sun to the items on the flaps to show how light travels and how it reacts in each situation. Under each flap, describe what happens.

7. Cut out the triangles flap. Apply glue to the back of the center section and attach it to the bottom of the page. Fold on dashed lines to create a tri-flap.

8. On the outside of the tri-flap, write *What happens when light enters a prism?* On the inside of the tri-flap, color the refraction lines to create a rainbow effect. Discuss how prisms bend light and separate white light into the separate colors.

Reflect on Learning

To complete the left-hand page, have students create a poster that explains reflected, refracted, and absorbed light. The poster should include graphic illustrations to explain how light reacts with matter.

Light

Light is a form of _____ that travels in a _____ _____ .
It can be _____ , _____ , or _____ .

the sun

reflect	refract	absorb

When light enters a prism, and separated into the colors.

it is refracted,

Transparent, Translucent, and Opaque

Introduction

Have students work in small groups to prepare the best way to send a secret message to a friend. Have one member of the group write a "secret" message on a piece of paper. Then, have students alternately cover it with a dark piece of construction paper, a piece of waxed paper, and a piece of clear plastic wrap. Discuss what happens with each material, which was best for concealing the message, and why.

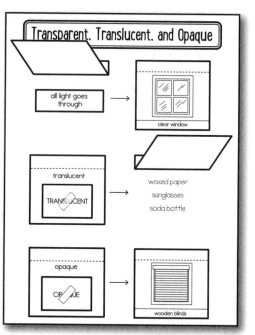

Creating the Notebook Page

Guide students through the following steps to complete the right-hand page in their notebooks.

1. Add a Table of Contents entry for the Transparent, Translucent, and Opaque pages.

2. Cut out the title and glue it to the top of the page.

3. Cut out the *transparent, translucent,* and *opaque* flaps.
   Apply glue to the back of the top sections and attach them to the left side of the page in a column.

4. Cut out the description pieces. Glue each piece under the appropriate flap (transparent: all light goes through; translucent: only some light goes through; opaque: no light goes through).

5. Cut out the *opaque, translucent, transparent* example pieces. Glue them on the flap of the appropriate term.

6. Cut out the picture flaps. Glue them to the right of the appropriate flap. Draw an arrow between each flap and its example.

7. Under these flaps, write more examples of each category.

Reflect on Learning

To complete the left-hand page, have students identify three classroom objects: one that is transparent, one that is translucent, and one that is opaque. Students should clearly label each object. Then, have students choose one item and explain why it is useful the way it is.

© Carson-Dellosa • CD-104908

Transparent, Translucent, and Opaque

all light goes through	transparent	translucent
no light goes through	opaque	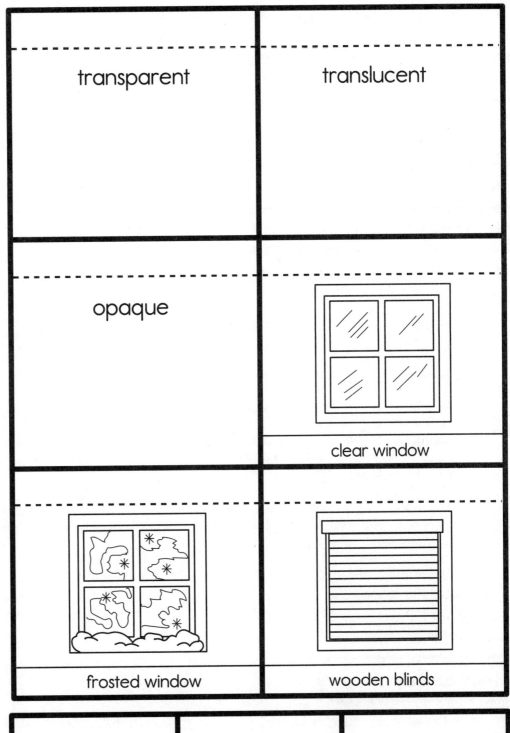clear window
only some light goes through	frosted window	wooden blinds

 OPAQUE    TRANSLUCENT    TRANSPARENT

Sound

Introduction

Fill a shallow container, such as a 9- by 12-inch glass baking dish, with water. Drop a few drops of water into the container. Ask students to observe what happens. Explain that the water ripples, or waves, created are similar to the sound waves that travel through the air. Then, ask students to place two fingers on the front of their throats and hum. Discuss how these vibrations travel in many directions through the air as waves. When the waves reach our ears, they make our eardrums vibrate too, which our brains translate as sound.

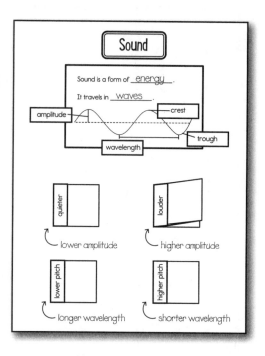

Creating the Notebook Page

Guide students through the following steps to complete the right-hand page in their notebooks.

1. Add a Table of Contents entry for the Sound pages.

2. Cut out the title and glue it to the top of the page.

3. Cut out the *Sound is* piece and glue it below the title.

4. Complete the explanation of sound. (Sound is a form of **energy**. It travels in **waves**.)

5. Cut out the *amplitude, crest, trough,* and *wavelength* labels. Glue the labels in the correct places to complete the diagram. You may want to draw lines on the diagram to better connect and label each part.

6. Cut out the four accordion folds. Fold on the dashed lines, alternating the fold direction. Apply glue to the back of the last sections of each and attach them in a two-by-two grid on the bottom half of the page.

7. Cut out the four remaining labels. Glue each label on the right side of the accordion fold to label the sound wave with the correct pitch or volume. If desired, describe the connection between the shape of the sound wave and its pitch or loudness on the page below the accordion fold.

Reflect on Learning

To complete the left-hand page, have students choose two common sounds and draw a sound wave for each sound. Students should explain how their sound waves match the sounds.

Sound

Sound is a form of _____.

It travels in _____.

crest	wavelength	louder	quieter
amplitude	trough	higher pitch	lower pitch

Electricity

Introduction

Demonstrate turning on and off a battery-operated flashlight. Explain how the switch on the flashlight controls the flow of electricity throughout the flashlight circuit. Explain that a circuit is simply a closed loop through which charges can continuously move.

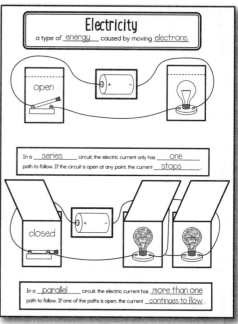

Creating the Notebook Page

Guide students through the following steps to complete the right-hand page in their notebooks.

1. Add a Table of Contents entry for the Electricity pages.

2. Cut out the title and glue it to the top of the page.

3. Complete the definition of electricity (a type of **energy** caused by moving **electrons**).

4. To create the series circuit, cut out an open and a closed switch flap. Label each one *open* or *closed*. Apply glue to the gray glue section of the closed switch and place the open switch on top to create a stacked two-flap book. Glue it to the left side of the page below the title. Then, cut out two of the lightbulb flaps, one with a gray glue section and one without. Apply glue to the gray glue section of the bottom lightbulb and place the other lightbulb on top. Glue it to the top right side of the page. Color one lightbulb yellow. Finally, cut out a battery piece and glue it between the two, slightly above the two other flaps. Draw lines (wires) to connect the series circuit.

5. To create the parallel circuit, repeat step 4, adding another lightbulb stacked flap book beside the first one. (Leave enough space below the first diagram to glue one of the circuit definition pieces.) Draw lines (wires) to connect the parallel circuit.

6. Cut out the two circuit definition pieces. Complete each definition. (In a **series** circuit, the electric current only has **one** path to follow. If the circuit is open at any point, the current **stops**. In a **parallel** circuit, the electric current has **more than one** path to follow. If one of the paths is open, the current **continues to flow**.) Then, glue each piece below the correct circuit diagram.

Reflect on Learning

To complete the left-hand page, have students describe why holiday lights are often created as parallel circuits. Students should draw a short string of holiday lights with one burnt out to show the flow of electricity through the string.

Electricity

a type of _____ caused by moving _____

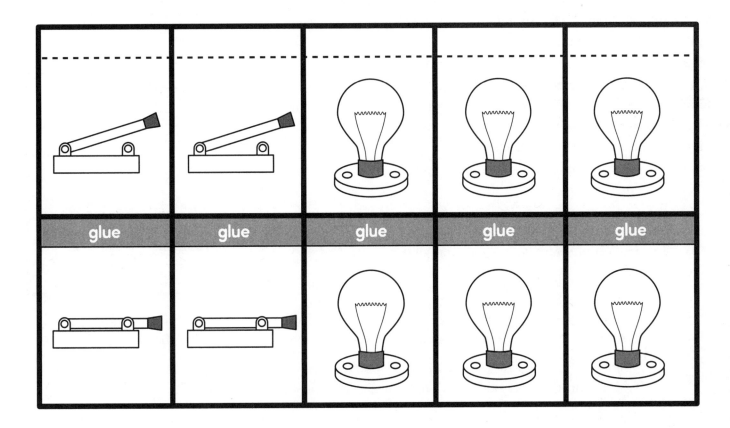

glue   glue   glue   glue   glue

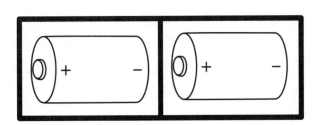

In a _____ circuit, the electric current only has _____ path to follow. If the circuit is open at any point, the current _____ .

In a _____ circuit, the electric current has _____ path to follow. If one of the paths is open, the current _____ .

Conductors and Insulators

Hold up a metal cooking spoon and a wooden cooking spoon. Discuss which one would be best to use when stirring a liquid in a pan on the stove. Then, ask what a cook might use to remove a hot pan from the oven and why.

Creating the Notebook Page

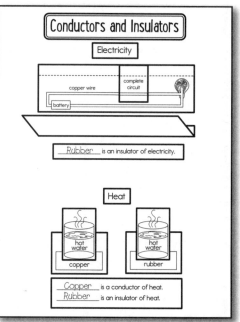

Guide students through the following steps to complete the right-hand page in their notebooks.

1. Add a Table of Contents entry for the Conductors and Insulators pages.

2. Cut out the title and glue it to the top of the page.

3. Cut out the *Electricity* label and glue it below the title.

4. Cut out the two *battery/bulb* flaps. Apply glue to the back of the top sections and attach them below the *Electricity* label. Cut out the two *complete circuit* flaps. Apply glue to the back of the top sections and attach them on the *battery/bulb* flaps over the spot where the circuit is broken.

5. Color the bulb that is now "lit." Discuss that the bulb is lit only on the circuit with the copper wire because it is a conductor, while rubber is an insulator.

6. Cut out the *conductor/insulator of electricity* pieces. Glue each under the correct flap.

7. Complete each sentence. (**Copper** is a conductor of electricity. **Rubber** is an insulator of electricity.)

8. Cut out the *Heat* label and glue it in the center of the page.

9. Cut out the *rubber* and *copper* pieces and glue them below the *Heat* label.

10. Discuss which of these would be a good conductor of heat and which would be a good insulator of heat.

11. Cut out the *hot water* pieces and glue them inside the *copper* and *rubber* pieces.

12. Cut out the *conductor/insulator of heat* piece and glue it to the bottom of the page.

13. Complete each sentence. (**Copper** is a conductor of heat. **Rubber** is an insulator of heat.)

Reflect on Learning

To complete the left-hand page, have students describe a way to insulate a cup of hot chocolate with supplies in their classroom.

Conductors and Insulators

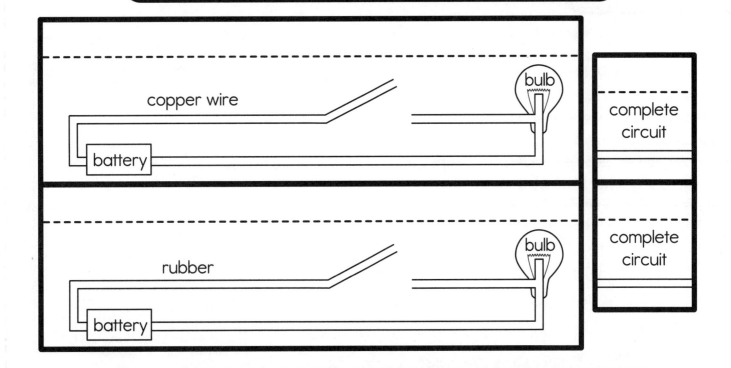

copper wire

battery

bulb

complete circuit

rubber

battery

bulb

complete circuit

Electricity | Heat

_____ is a conductor of electricity.

_____ is an insulator of electricity.

_____ is a conductor of heat.

_____ is an insulator of heat.

hot water

hot water

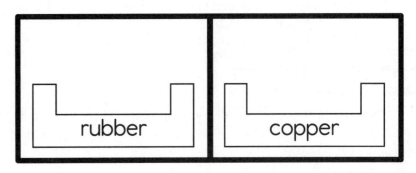

rubber

copper

Magnets

Introduction

Break students into groups of four to act out magnet "interactions." Have each pair of students in the group act as a magnet, with one student acting as the north pole and the other as the south pole. Offer different scenarios, such as north to north or north to south and have the groups act them out. Discuss what the interactions are in each case.

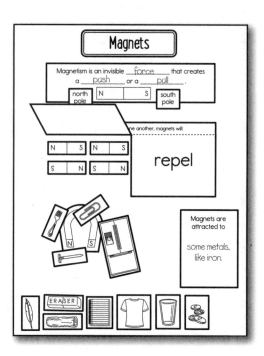

Creating the Notebook Page

Guide students through the following steps to complete the right-hand page in their notebooks.

1. Add a Table of Contents entry for the Magnets pages.

2. Cut out the title and glue it to the top of the page.

3. Cut the *Magnetism is* piece and glue it below the title.

4. Complete the definition. (Magnetism is an invisible **force** that creates a **push** or a **pull**.)

5. Cut out the *north pole* and *south pole* labels. Discuss the parts of a magnet. Glue the labels to the magnet on the *Magnetism is* piece to label the poles.

6. Cut out the flap book. Cut on the solid line to create two flaps. Apply glue to the back of the top section and attach it to the page below the *Magnetism is* piece.

7. Cut out the eight bar magnets. Glue them under the *attract* and *repel* flaps to show the different situations or arrangements in which magnets attract and repel each other.

8. Cut out the horseshoe magnet and glue it below the flap book.

9. Cut out the objects. Glue the objects that are attracted to magnets to the horseshoe magnet. Glue the objects that are not attracted to magnets to the very bottom of the page. If possible, test real-life versions of each object with a magnet to see if it is attracted to a magnet.

10. Cut out the *Magnets are attracted to* piece and glue it to the bottom right of the page.

11. Discuss what magnets are attracted to, and complete the sentence. (Magnets are attracted to **some metals, like iron**.)

Reflect on Learning

To complete the left-hand page, have students list items found in their homes that use magnets.

Magnets

Magnetism is an invisible _____ that creates a _____ or a _____ .

| N | S |

When placed beside one another, magnets will:

attract

repel

| north pole | south pole |

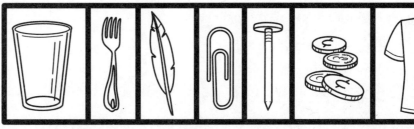

S	S	S	S
N	N	N	N
S	S	S	S
N	N	N	N

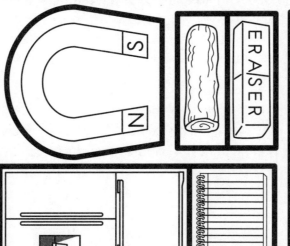

ERASER

Magnets are attracted to

Forces

Introduction

Have students make ramps by placing one or more books under one end of a piece of cardboard. Allow each student to gently push a toy car down the ramp. Then, have students test ways to make their cars travel faster or go farther. Discuss the forces at work on the car. Ask questions such as, *What makes it move toward the bottom of the ramp? What keeps it from moving faster?* Discuss the effects of gravity and friction on the toy cars.

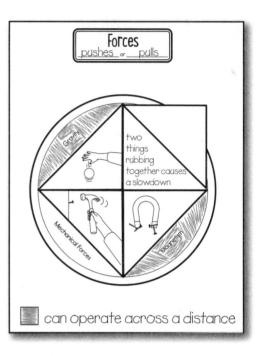

Creating the Notebook Page

Guide students through the following steps to complete the right-hand page in their notebooks.

1. Add a Table of Contents entry for the Forces pages.

2. Cut out the title and glue it to the top of the page.

3. Complete the description of forces (**pushes** or **pulls**).

4. Cut out the circle piece. Fold it in half horizontally along one of the solid lines with the text on the outside. Cut on that solid line. Unfold and fold it in half vertically. Cut on the that solid line. Be careful not to cut all the way through the outer edge. The circle will have four triangular flaps in its center. Apply glue to the back of the outside edge of the circle and attach it to the center of the page.

5. Cut out the picture pieces. Discuss the different types of forces. Glue the picture pieces on the correct flaps.

6. Describe the force under each flap.

7. Color the name section of each flap that shows a force that can operate across a distance. Include a color key at the bottom of the page.

Reflect on Learning

To complete the left-hand page, have students draw lines to divide their pages into four sections. Label each section *Gravity, Friction, Magnetism,* and *Mechanical Forces*. Provide students with magazines and newspapers. Students should find and cut out pictures that demonstrate each type of force and glue them into the correct sections.

Forces

or _____

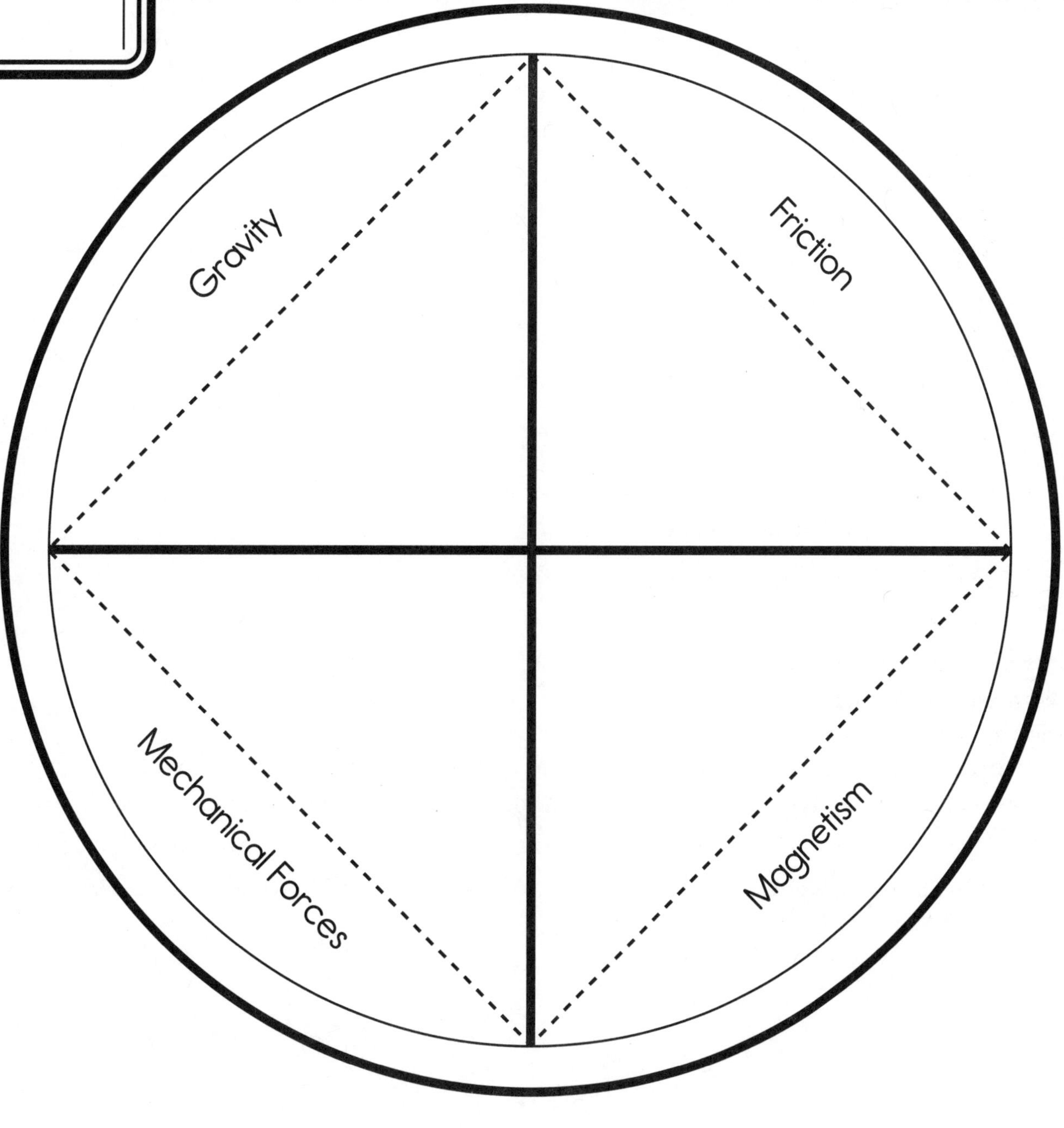

Gravity

Friction

Mechanical Forces

Magnetism

Rock Types

Introduction

Review with students the three types of rock. Have students use root words to better understand rock names (metamorphic, similar to metamorphosis of butterflies, meaning change; igneous: from fire; sedimentary: from sediments).

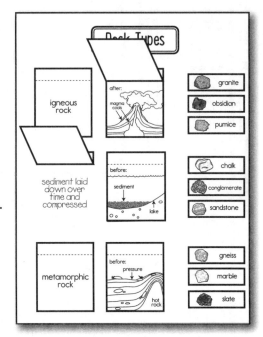

Creating the Notebook Page

Guide students through the following steps to complete the right-hand page in their notebooks.

1. Add a Table of Contents entry for the Rock Types pages.

2. Cut out the title and glue it to the top of the page.

3. Cut out the three flaps in the row beginning with *igneous rock*. Cut the flaps apart. Apply glue to the back of the top section of the *igneous rock* flap and attach it to the top left side of the page below the title.

4. Apply glue to the gray glue section of the *after* flap and place the *before* flap directly on top to create a stacked flap book. Then, glue the flap book to the right of the *igneous rock* flap.

5. Repeat steps 3 and 4 with the remaining two rows of flaps, creating a 2 by 3 grid.

6. Review each before-and-after flap book and discuss how each type of rock is formed. Under each *rock* flap book, write a description of how that type of rock is formed (igneous: from fire; sedimentary: sediment laid down over time and compacted; metamorphic: existing rock transformed by pressure and heat).

7. Cut out the rock pieces. Glue them to the right side of the page next to the correct type of rock.

Reflect on Learning

To complete the left-hand page, have students pretend they are newspaper reporters on the scene to describe first hand how the types of rock are being formed. Students should write an article.

Answer Key
igneous rock: granite, obsidian, pumice; sedimentary rock: chalk, conglomerate, sandstone; metamorphic rock: gneiss, marble, slate

Rock Types

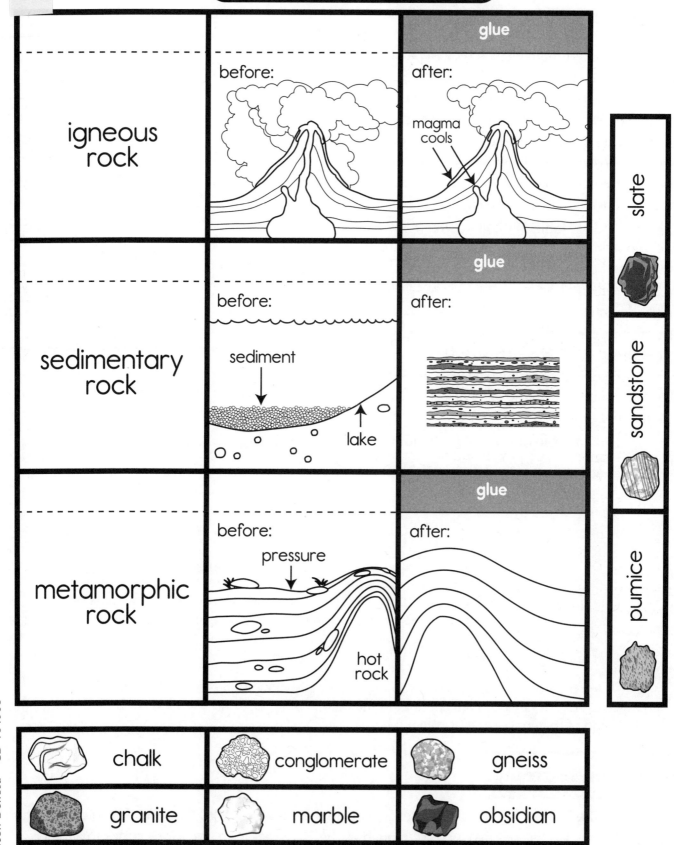

igneous rock	before:	glue after: magma cools
sedimentary rock	before: sediment / lake	glue after:
metamorphic rock	before: pressure / hot rock	glue after:

slate

sandstone

pumice

chalk	conglomerate	gneiss
granite	marble	obsidian

The Rock Cycle

To demonstrate the rock cycle, grate three colors of crayon wax onto a paper plate, keeping the colors separate. Explain that this represents weathering and erosion. Sprinkle a layer of each color into a small piece of tin foil. Describe this as depositing sediments. Fold the foil and apply intense pressure to demonstrate the pressure that creates sedimentary rock. Unfold the foil and show the "sedimentary rock." Fold the foil again and heat it by placing it in very hot water for a few moments. Then, carefully remove it and press firmly on it again to demonstrate the heat and extreme pressure that creates metamorphic rock. Show the "metamorphic rock." Fold the foil again and place it in very hot water, long enough for the crayon to melt completely. Remove it carefully. Open the foil and let it cool completely. Explain that the melted and cooled crayon represents igneous rock.

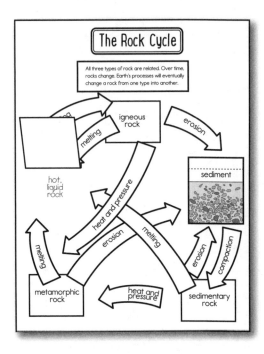

Creating the Notebook Page

Guide students through the following steps to complete the right-hand page in their notebooks.

1. Add a Table of Contents entry for the The Rock Cycle pages.

2. Cut out the title and glue it to the top of the page.

3. Cut out the explanation piece. Glue it below the title.

4. Cut out all of the other pieces, which will be used to illustrate the rock cycle. Color code the arrows if you wish.

5. Lay out all of the pieces in the correct positions to be sure they fit before gluing them to the page. Place the three types of rock pieces in a triangular formation beginning with the *igneous rock* piece at the center top, the *sedimentary rock* piece on the bottom right, and the *metamorphic rock* piece on the lower left. Place the *magma* and *sediment* flaps on the center left and right sides of the page.

6. Glue the rock and arrow pieces to the page. Apply glue to the back of the top sections of each of the flaps and attach them to the page. Under each flap, write a short definition of the type of material.

Reflect on Learning

To complete the left-hand page, have students imagine that they are rocks. Students should create comic strips describing the changes they will go through as they progress from one form of rock to another.

The Rock Cycle

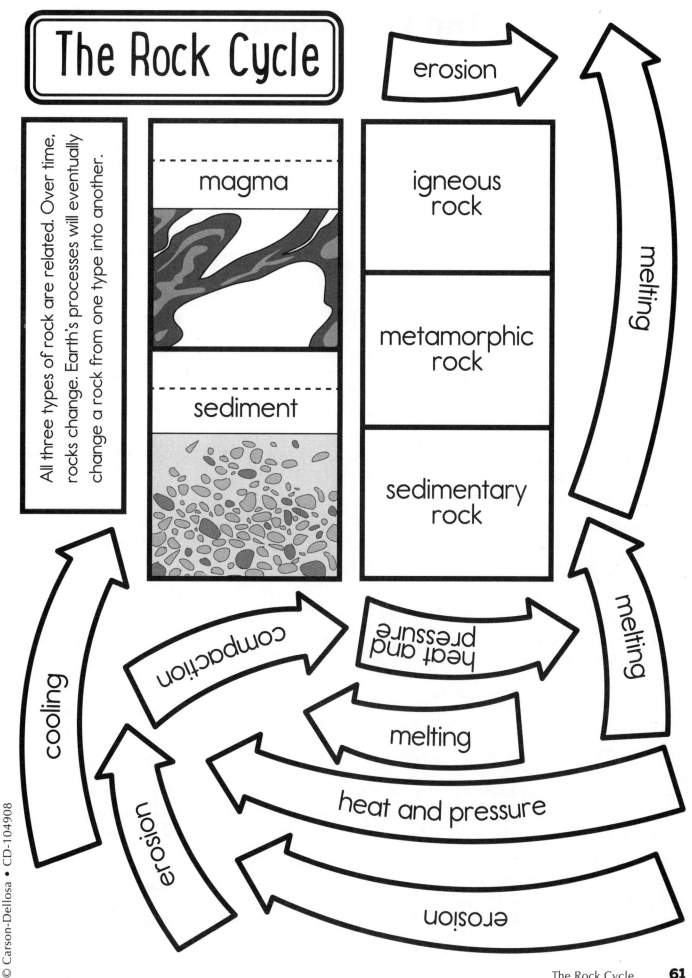

All three types of rock are related. Over time, rocks change. Earth's processes will eventually change a rock from one type into another.

magma

sediment

igneous rock

metamorphic rock

sedimentary rock

erosion

melting

melting

cooling

erosion

compaction

heat and pressure

melting

heat and pressure

erosion

Weathering and Erosion

Introduction

Have students discuss a place in their area where there has been new construction. Describe how things have changed. Relate this to how rock changes, mostly over long periods of time.

Creating the Notebook Page

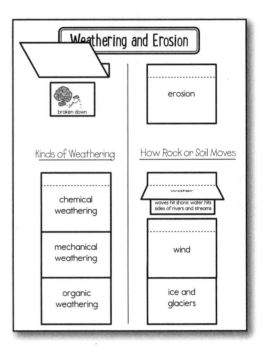

Guide students through the following steps to complete the right-hand page in their notebooks.

1. Add a Table of Contents entry for the Weathering and Erosion pages.

2. Cut out the title and glue it to the top of the page.

3. Cut out the *weathering* and *erosion* flaps. Apply glue to the back of the top sections and glue them side by side below the title.

4. Cut out the two picture pieces. Discuss the difference between weathering and erosion. Glue the correct picture under each flap.

5. Draw a vertical line below and between the *weathering* and *erosion* flaps to divide the page in half and create a T-chart. Below the *weathering* flap, write *Kinds of Weathering*. Below the *erosion* flap, write *How Rock or Soil Moves*.

6. Cut out the *chemical weathering*, *mechanical weathering*, and *organic weathering* flaps. Apply glue to the back of the top sections and attach them below the *weathering* flap.

7. Cut out the *water, wind,* and *ice and glaciers* flaps. Apply glue to the back of the top sections and attach them below the *Erosion* flap.

8. Cut out the description pieces.

9. Read each description and glue it under the correct flap in the T-chart.

Reflect on Learning

To complete the left-hand page, have students make Venn diagrams comparing and contrasting weathering and erosion.

Answer Key
chemical weathering: water dissolves limestone; mechanical weathering: freezing and thawing breaks rocks; organic weathering: plant roots and lichen break up rock; water: rain carries soil away; waves hit shore; water hits sides of rivers and streams; wind: wind carries particles; ice and glaciers: moving glaciers carry rocks

Weathering and Erosion

broken down

moved away

chemical weathering	water
organic weathering	wind
mechanical weathering	ice and glaciers
weathering	erosion

wind carries particles	plant roots and lichen break up rock
moving glaciers carry rocks	freezing and thawing breaks rocks
rain carries soil away; waves hit shore; water hits sides of rivers and streams	water dissolves limestone

Fossils

Introduction

Have the class brainstorm everything they know about fossils. Make lists on the board. Discuss what can become fossils (animals: dinosaurs, insects, mammals, and birds; plants; and animal tracks). Explain that fossils are the remains or impressions left behind from a plant or animal from a different geologic period.

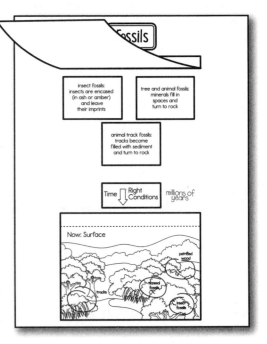

Creating the Notebook Page

Guide students through the following steps to complete the right-hand page in their notebooks.

1. Add a Table of Contents entry for the Fossils pages.

2. Cut out the title and glue it to the top of the page.

3. Cut out the *Then* flap. Apply glue to the back of the top section and attach it below the title.

4. Cut out the *Time* piece and glue it below the *Then* flap.

5. Cut out the three fossil description pieces and glue them under the *Then* flap.

6. Discuss how different types of fossils are formed. Beside the *Time* piece, write *millions of years*.

7. Cut out the *Now* flap. Apply glue to the back of the top section and attach it to the bottom of the page.

8. Cut out the *Now: underground* piece and glue it under the *Now* flap.

9. Circle and label the location of the "unseen" fossils on the *Now* flap.

Reflect on Learning

To complete the left-hand page, have students write a newspaper article about what scientists learned about the environment of the living things found as fossils on the *Now* flap.

Fossils

tree and animal fossils:
minerals fill in
spaces and
turn to rock

animal track fossils:
tracks become
filled with sediment
and turn to rock

insect fossils:
insects are encased
(in ash or amber)
and leave
their imprints

Time → Right Conditions

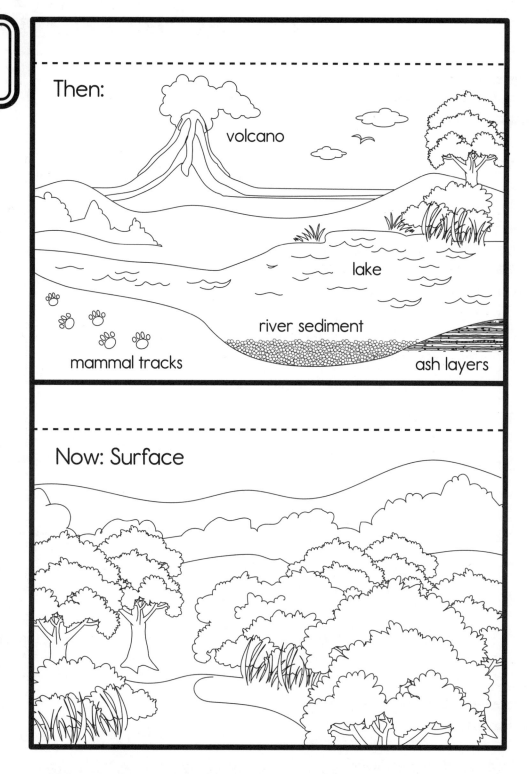

Then:

volcano

lake

river sediment

mammal tracks

ash layers

Now: Surface

Now: Underground

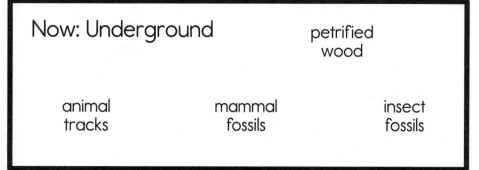

petrified wood

animal tracks

mammal fossils

insect fossils

Natural Disasters

Introduction

Display pictures of natural disasters. Place students in small groups and have each group create a poster describing a natural disaster such as an earthquake, volcano, or flood. Allow groups to share their posters with the rest of the class.

Creating the Notebook Page

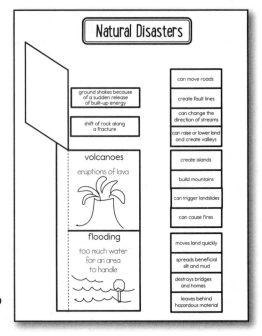

Guide students through the following steps to complete the right-hand page in their notebooks.

1. Add a Table of Contents entry for the Natural Disasters pages.

2. Cut out the title and glue it to the top of the page.

3. Cut out the *earthquakes, volcanoes, flooding* flap book. Cut on the solid lines to create three flaps. Apply glue to the back of the left side and attach it to the left side of the page.

4. On each flap, draw and write a short description of the natural disaster.

5. Cut out the six description pieces and glue them under the appropriate flaps. (Earthquakes: ground shakes because of a sudden release of built-up energy; shift of rock along a fracture; Volcanoes: can release gases, ash, and lava; tend to exist near the edges of tectonic plates; Flooding: cause more property damage than any other natural disaster; can be due to precipitation, earthquakes, or volcanic activity)

6. Cut out the 12 changes pieces. Glue each piece to the right of the natural disaster that can cause that change in the earth. (Note: Some changes may be caused by more than one natural disaster or may not be caused every time the natural disaster occurs.)

Reflect on Learning

To complete the left-hand page, have students create triple Venn diagrams comparing and contrasting earthquakes, volcanoes, and floods.

Answer Key
Some answers may apply to more than one natural disaster. Earthquakes: can move roads, create fault lines, can change the direction of streams, can raise or lower land and create valleys; volcanoes: create islands, build mountains, can trigger landslides, can cause fires; flooding: move land quickly, spread beneficial silt and mud, destroy bridges and homes, leave behind hazardous material

Natural Disasters

earthquakes

volcanoes

flooding

ground shakes because of a sudden release of built-up energy	
shift of rock along a fracture	
can release gases, ash, and lava	
tend to exist near the edges of tectonic plates	
cause more property damage than any other natural disaster	
can be due to precipitation, earthquakes, or volcanic activity	

build mountains	create islands
can cause fires	create fault lines
can change the direction of streams	destroys bridges and homes
can move roads	leaves behind hazardous material
can raise or lower land and create valleys	moves land quickly
can trigger landslides	spreads beneficial silt and mud

Earth's Water

Have students list every time they used water today from when they woke up to the current moment. As a class, compare lists and discuss how water affects students' lives.

Creating the Notebook Page

Guide students through the following steps to complete the right-hand page in their notebooks.

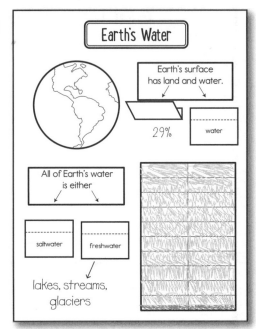

1. Add a Table of Contents entry for the Earth's Water pages.

2. Cut out the title and glue it on the top of the page.

3. Cut out the image of Earth and glue it on the upper left part of the page.

4. Cut out the *Earth's surface* piece and glue it to the right of the Earth piece.

5. Cut out the *land* and *water* flaps. Apply glue to the back of the top sections and attach them below the arrows on the *Earth's surface* piece.

6. Under the *land* flap, write *29%*. Discuss that 29 percent of Earth's surface is covered by land. Under the *water* flap, write *71%*. Discuss that 71 percent of Earth's surface is covered by water.

7. Cut out the *All of Earth's water* piece and glue it to the page below the Earth piece.

8. Cut out the *saltwater* and *freshwater* flaps. Apply glue to the back of the top sections and attach them below the arrows on the *All of Earth's water* piece.

9. Under the *saltwater* flap, write *96.5%*. Discuss that of all of the water on Earth, 96.5 percent of it is saltwater. Under the *freshwater* flap, write *3.5%*. Discuss that of all of the water on Earth, only 3.5 percent of it is freshwater.

10. Cut out the grid and glue it to the bottom right side of the page. Color 96.5% of the space using one color to indicate the percent of saltwater on Earth. Color the remaining 3.5% a different color to represent freshwater.

11. Below the *freshwater* flaps, write examples of where freshwater can be found on Earth.

To complete the left-hand page, have students create posters to promote water conservation. Posters should include reasons explaining why people should conserve water.

Earth's Water

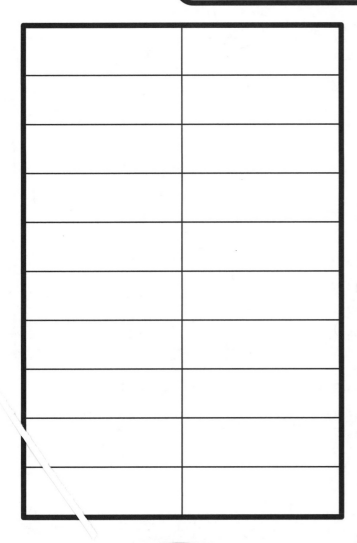

Earth's surface has land and water.

All of Earth's water is either

| land | water |
| saltwater | freshwater |

The Moon's Phases

Have students work in small groups to draw some of the phases of the moon. Have groups share their phases. As a class, place the phases in order and try to identify and add any missing phases.

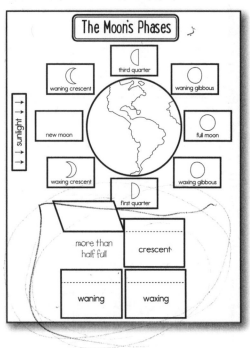

Creating the Notebook Page

Guide students through the following steps to complete the right-hand page in their notebooks.

1. Add a Table of Contents entry for the The Moon's Phases pages.

2. Cut out the title and glue it to the top of the page.

3. Cut out *sunlight* piece and glue it to the left of the page so that the arrows are pointing from the left.

4. Cut out the Earth piece and glue it vertically to the middle of the page.

5. Cut out the moon pieces. Glue them in the correct positions around the Earth piece.

6. Cut out the *gibbous, crescent, waning,* and *waxing* flaps. Apply glue to the back of the top sections and attach them to the bottom of the page.

7. Under each flap, write the meaning of the term.

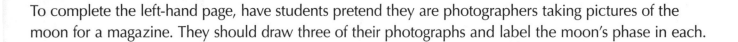

To complete the left-hand page, have students pretend they are photographers taking pictures of the moon for a magazine. They should draw three of their photographs and label the moon's phase in each.

The Moon's Phases

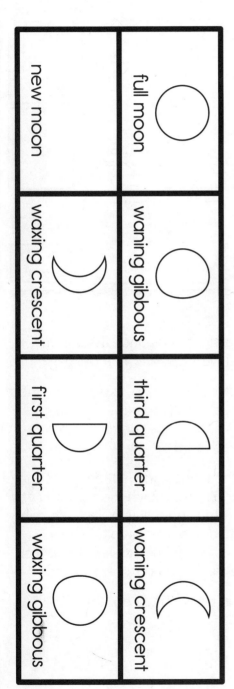

gibbous	crescent
waning	waxing

Movement of the Sun, Stars, and Earth

Introduction

Draw a sun on the board and write the word *sun* in the center. Ask students to brainstorm everything they know about the sun. Write students' responses on the board around the sun. Review that the sun is the center of the solar system and that the planets orbit around it. The sun's position is like the hub of a bicycle wheel, with planets spinning around it counterclockwise.

Creating the Notebook Page

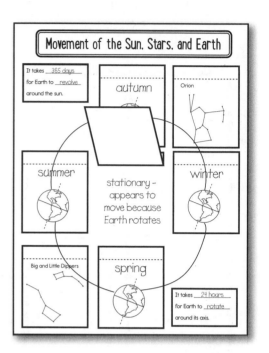

Guide students through the following steps to complete the right-hand page in their notebooks.

1. Add a Table of Contents entry for the Movement of the Sun, Stars, and Earth pages.

2. Cut out the title and glue it to the top of the page.

3. Cut out the *sun* flap. Apply glue to the back of the top section and attach it to the center of the page.

4. Cut out the Earth flaps. Apply glue to the back of the top sections and attach them in the proper positions around the sun in a north, east, south, and west formation on the page.

5. Draw a line to show Earth's revolution around the sun. Under the sun flap, explain why the sun is stationary but appears to move (due to Earth's daily rotation). Under the Earth flaps, describe seasonal changes due to the tilt of Earth on its axis and its position relative to the sun. Write the season for the northern hemisphere above each Earth.

6. Cut out the *Orion* and *Big and Little Dipper* flaps. Apply glue to the back of the top section of each. Attach the *Orion* flap between the north and east Earth flaps. Attach the *Big and Little Dippers* flap between the south and west Earth flaps. Under the constellation flaps, describe the "movement" of the stars (they don't move, but appear to due to Earth's rotation and revolution) and the change in visible constellations. (Orion is seen in the late fall and winter months, and the Big and Little Dippers are best seen in the spring and summer months.)

7. Cut out the *It takes* pieces. Glue each one in the top left and bottom right positions on the page.

8. Complete the text on each flap. (It takes **365 days** for Earth to **revolve** around the sun. It takes **24 hours** for Earth to **rotate** around its axis.)

Reflect on Learning

To complete the left-hand page, have students write lesson plans to explain the movement of the sun, stars, and Earth to a first grader.

Movement of the Sun, Stars, and Earth

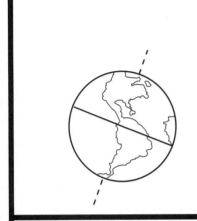

It takes _____ _____

for Earth to _____

around the sun.

It takes _____ _____

for Earth to _____

around its axis.

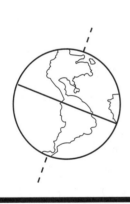

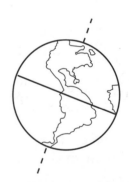

Orion

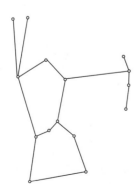

Big and Little Dippers

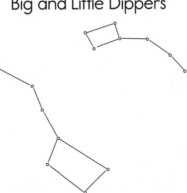

the sun

Weather and Climate

Introduction

Have students discuss a time when the weather forecast was wrong. Discuss how it affected their plans and why the meteorologist might have been wrong. Compare last week's forecast and the actual weather. How far off was the forecast? Can students guess what next week's weather might be like generally? Why or why not?

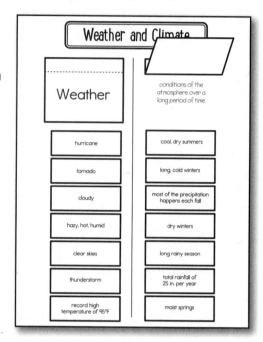

Creating the Notebook Page

Guide students through the following steps to complete the right-hand page in their notebooks.

1. Add a Table of Contents entry for the Weather and Climate pages.

2. Cut out the title and glue it to the top of the page.

3. Cut out the *Weather* and *Climate* flaps. Apply glue to the back of the top sections and attach them side by side below the title.

4. Under each flap, describe each term. (Weather: conditions of the atmosphere over a short period of time; Climate: conditions of the atmosphere over a long period of time)

5. Cut out the 14 description pieces. Draw a vertical line down the page to divide the page in half between the *Weather* and *Climate* flaps.

6. Read each piece and decide whether it is describing weather or climate. Glue it to the page below the correct flap.

Reflect on Learning

To complete the left-hand page, have students describe the climate and the weather of their location over the last few days. Then, students should create Venn diagrams to compare weather and climate.

Answer Key
Weather: clear skies; cloudy; hazy, hot, humid; hurricane; record high temperature of 95°F; thunderstorm; tornado
Climate: cool, dry summers; dry winters; long, cold winters; long rainy season; moist springs; most of the precipitation happens each fall; total rainfall of 25 in. per year

Weather and Climate

Weather	Climate
hurricane	clear skies
cool, dry summers	dry winters
long, cold winters	long rainy season
most of the precipitation happens each fall	record high temperature of 95°F
tornado	total rainfall of 25 in. per year
cloudy	moist springs
hazy, hot, humid	thunderstorm

Renewable and Nonrenewable Energy Sources

Each student will need a brass paper fastener to complete this page.

Introduction

Have a student turn off the lights and another student turn them back on. Discuss where the energy comes from that supplies the school with electricity. Provide students with small self-stick notes. Then, have students place self-stick notes on all of the items in the classroom that need energy to function. Explain that energy use is an integral part of our lives and that there are many different sources of energy.

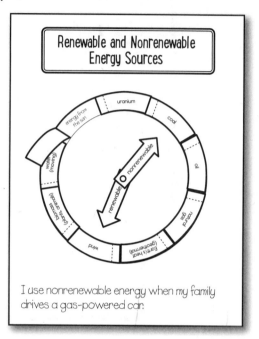

Creating the Notebook Page

Guide students through the following steps to complete the right-hand page in their notebooks.

1. Add a Table of Contents entry for the Renewable and Nonrenewable Energy Sources pages.

2. Cut out the title and glue it to the top of the page.

3. Cut out the large circle and the two arrows. Place the arrows on top of the circle with the *nonrenewable* arrow on top. Push a brass paper fastener through the center dots to connect the circle and arrows. It may be helpful to create the hole in each piece separately first. Apply glue to the back of the circle and glue it below the title. The brass paper fastener should not go through the page and both arrows should spin freely.

4. Cut out the flaps. Apply glue to the back of the left section of the flaps and attach them to the spaces around the large circle.

5. Under each flap, describe each energy source. For example, solar power is energy from the sun.

6. Spin the arrows to tell if each source is renewable or nonrenewable.

7. At the bottom of the page, explain a way that you use one of the above energy types in your life. Tell if it is renewable or nonrenewable energy.

Reflect on Learning

To complete the left-hand page, have students write letters to people who do not care about wasting energy. They should try to convince the letter recipients to change their ways of thinking.

Renewable and Nonrenewable Energy Sources

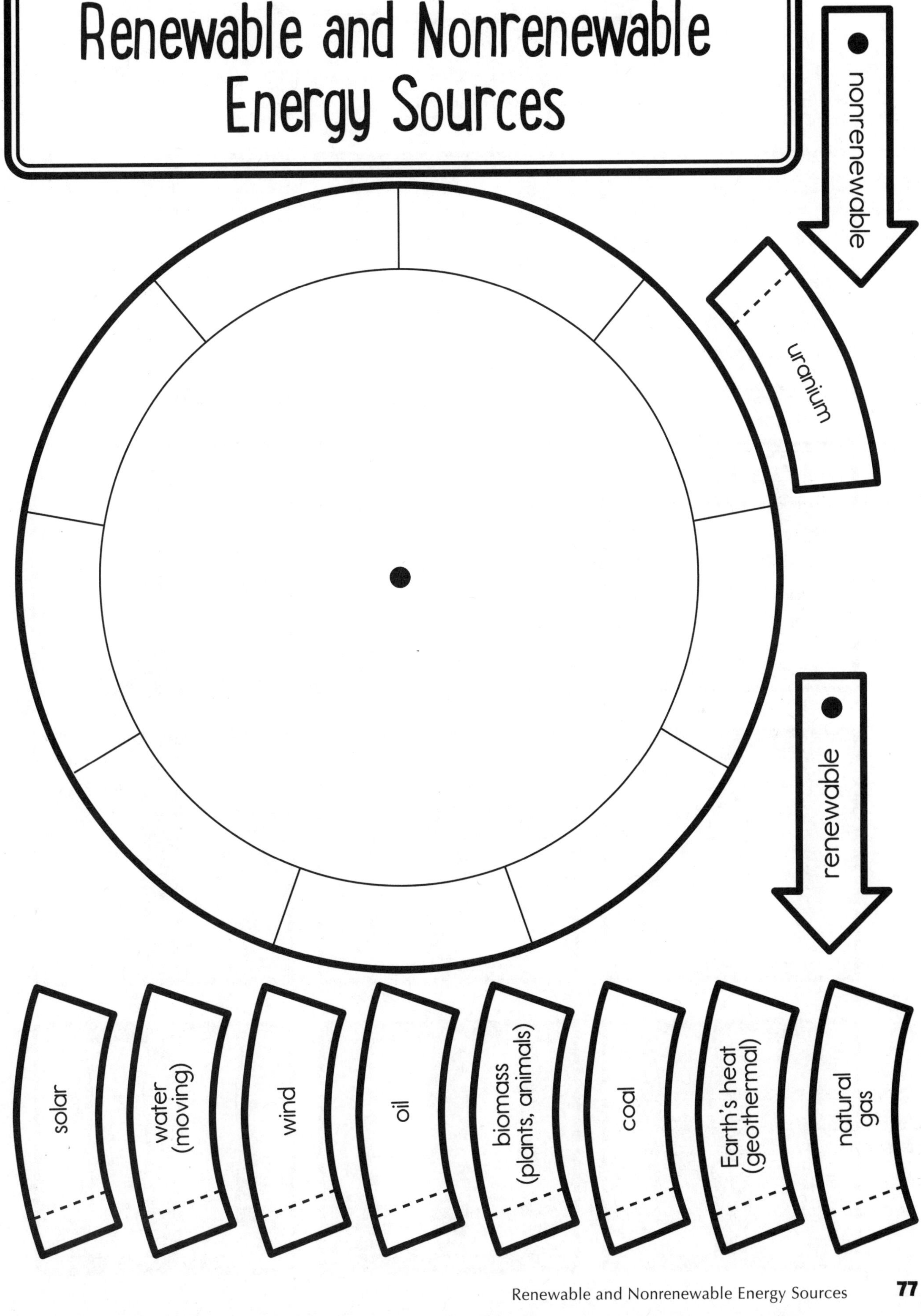

nonrenewable

uranium

renewable

solar

water (moving)

wind

oil

biomass (plants, animals)

coal

Earth's heat (geothermal)

natural gas

Tabs

Cut out each tab and label it. Apply glue to the back of each tab and align it on the outside edge of the page with only the label section showing beyond the edge. Then, fold each tab to seal the page inside.

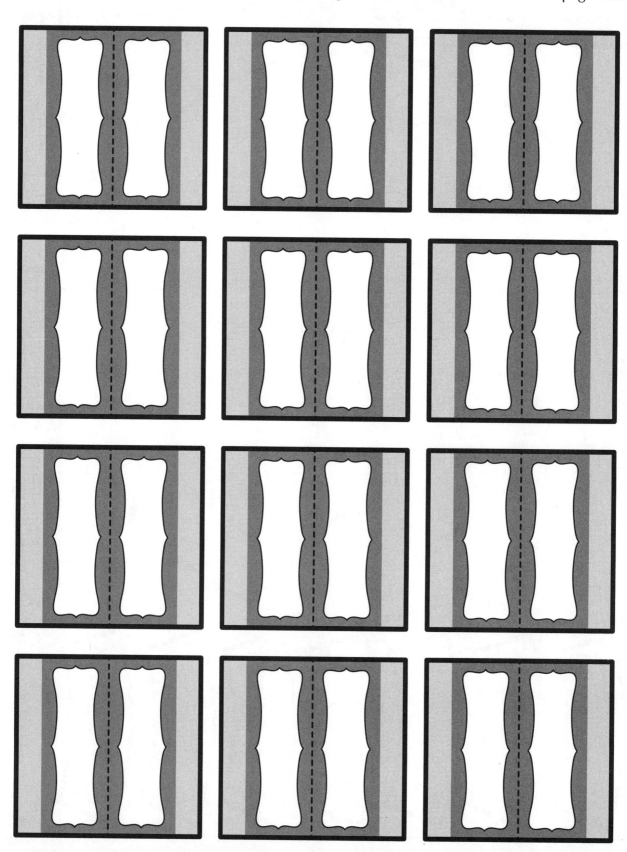

Cut out the KWL chart and cut on the solid lines to create three separate flaps. Apply glue to the back of the Topic section to attach the chart to a notebook page.

What I

Know

What I

Wonder

What I

Learned

Topic:

Library Pocket

Cut out the library pocket on the solid lines. Fold in the side tabs and apply glue to them before folding up the front of the pocket. Apply glue to the back of the pocket to attach it to a notebook page.

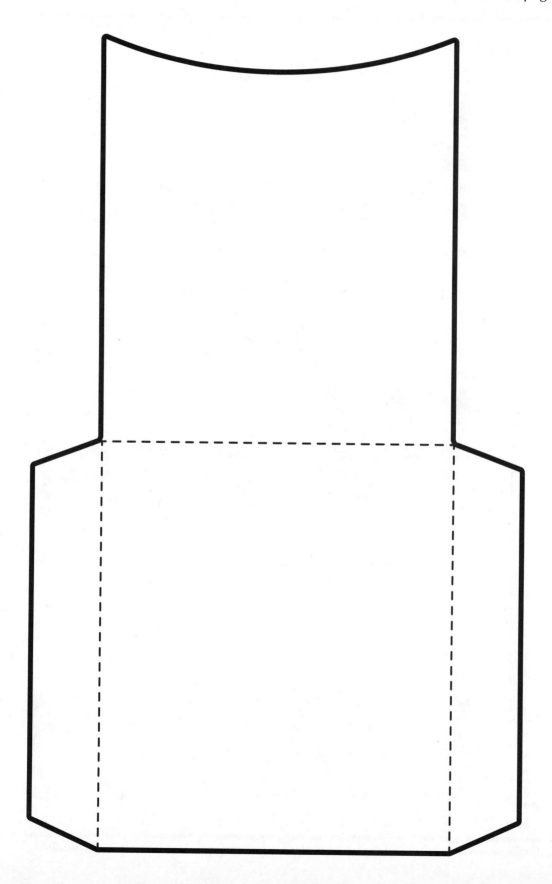

Envelope

Cut out the envelope on the solid lines. Fold in the side tabs and apply glue to them before folding up the rectangular front of the envelope. Fold down the triangular flap to close the envelope. Apply glue to the back of the envelope to attach it to a notebook page.

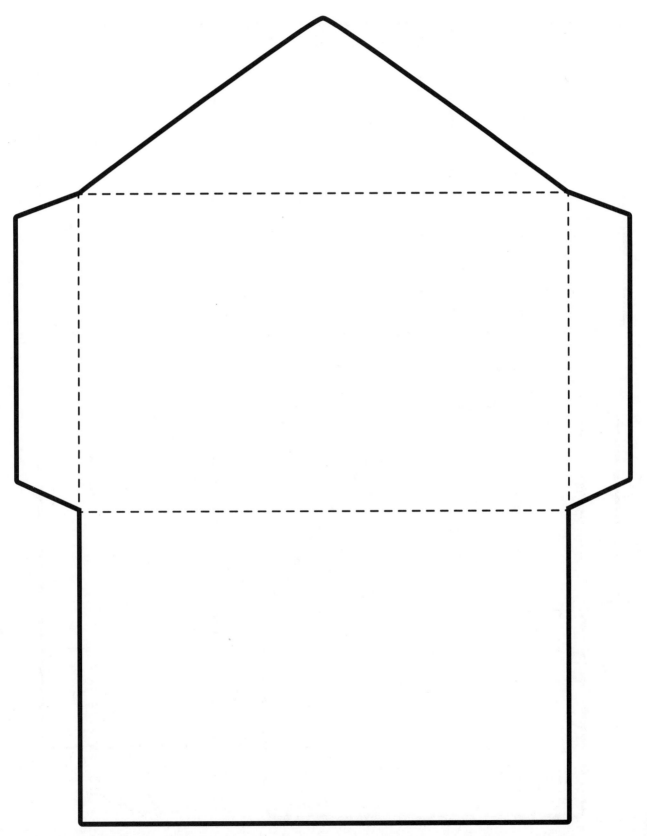

Pocket and Cards

Cut out the pocket on the solid lines. Fold over the front of the pocket. Then, apply glue to the tabs and fold them around the back of the pocket. Apply glue to the back of the pocket to attach it to a notebook page. Cut out the cards and store them in the envelope.

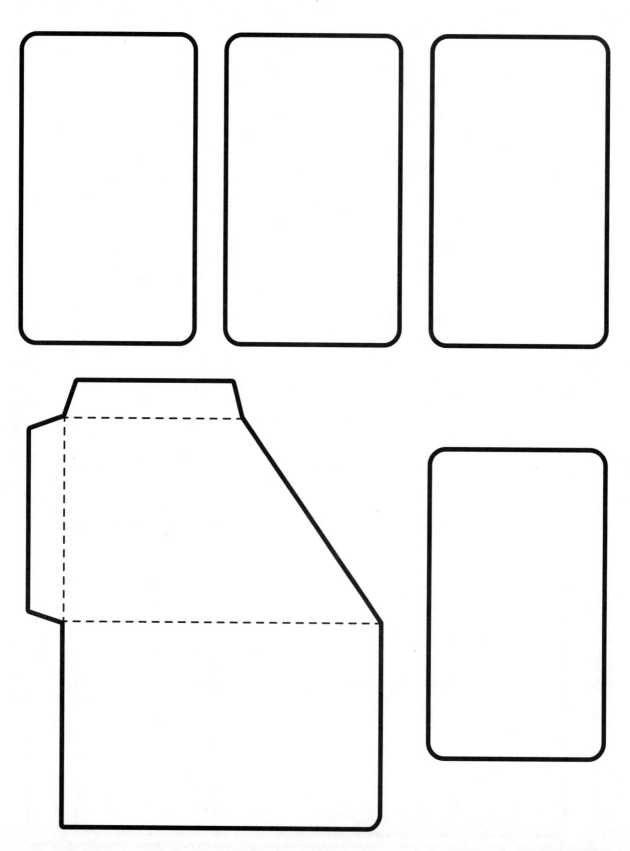

Six-Flap Shutter Fold

Cut out the shutter fold around the outside border. Then, cut on the solid lines to create six flaps. Fold the flaps toward the center. Apply glue to the back of the shutter fold to attach it to a notebook page.

If desired, this template can be modified to create a four-flap shutter fold by cutting off the bottom row. You can also create two three-flap books by cutting it in half down the center line.

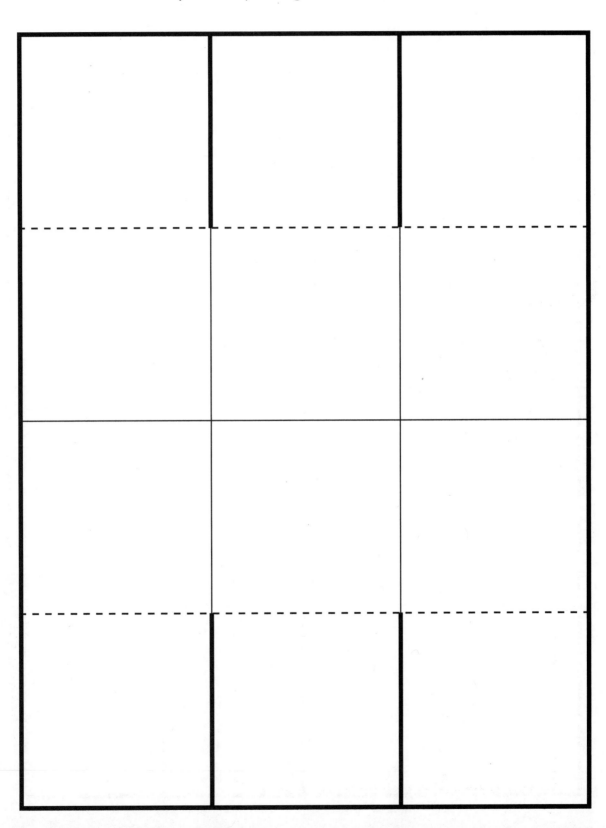

Eight-Flap Shutter Fold

Cut out the shutter fold around the outside border. Then, cut on the solid lines to create eight flaps. Fold the flaps toward the center. Apply glue to the back of the shutter fold to attach it to a notebook page.

If desired, this template can be modified to create two four-flap shutter folds by cutting off the bottom two rows. You can also create two four-flap books by cutting it in half down the center line.

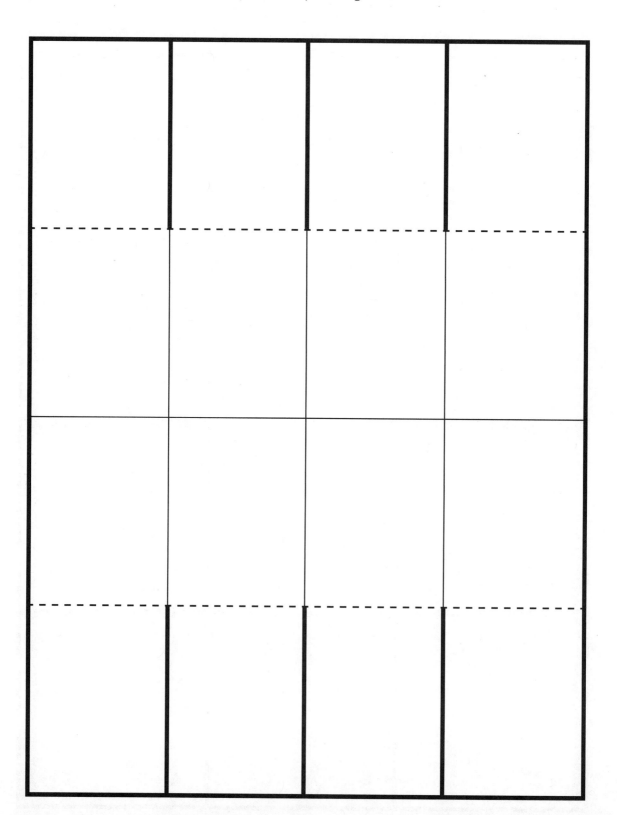

Flap Book—Eight Flaps

Cut out the flap book around the outside border. Then, cut on the solid lines to create eight flaps. Apply glue to the back of the center section to attach it to a notebook page.

If desired, this template can be modified to create a six-flap or two four-flap books by cutting off the bottom row or two. You can also create a tall four-flap book by cutting off the flaps on the left side.

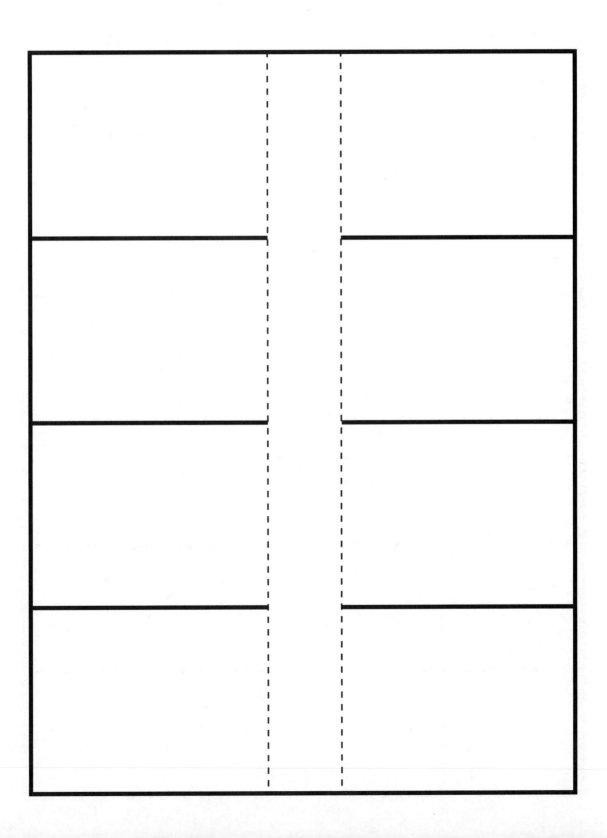

Flap Book—Twelve Flaps

Cut out the flap book around the outside border. Then, cut on the solid lines to create 12 flaps. Apply glue to the back of the center section to attach it to a notebook page.

If desired, this template can be modified to create smaller flap books by cutting off any number of rows from the bottom. You can also create a tall flap book by cutting off the flaps on the left side.

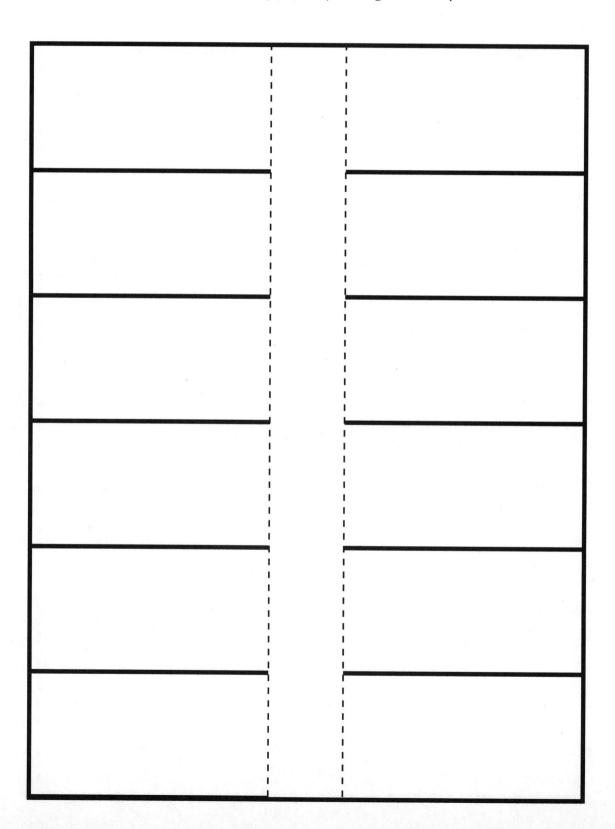

Shaped Flaps

Cut out each shaped flap. Apply glue to the back of the narrow section to attach it to a notebook page.

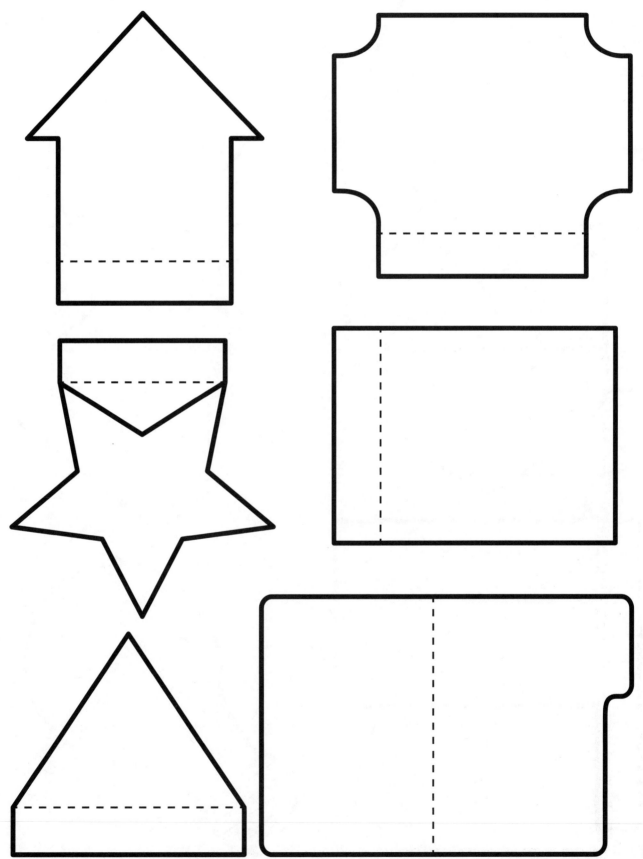

Shaped Flaps

Interlocking Booklet

Cut out the booklet on the solid lines, including the short vertical lines on the top and bottom flaps. Then, fold the top and bottom flaps toward the center, interlocking them using the small vertical cuts. Apply glue to the back of the center panel to attach it to a notebook page.

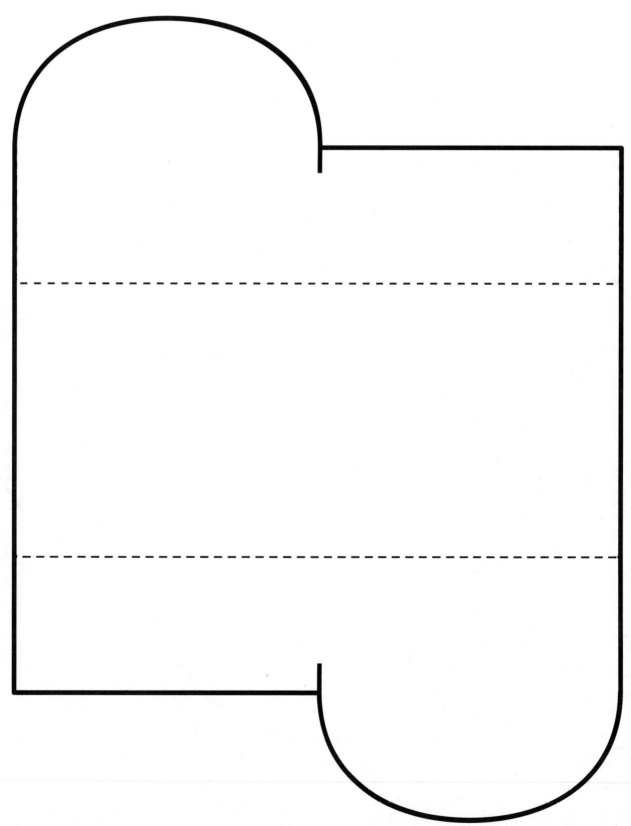

Four-Flap Petal Fold

Cut out the shape on the solid lines. Then, fold the flaps toward the center. Apply glue to the back of the center panel to attach it to a notebook page.

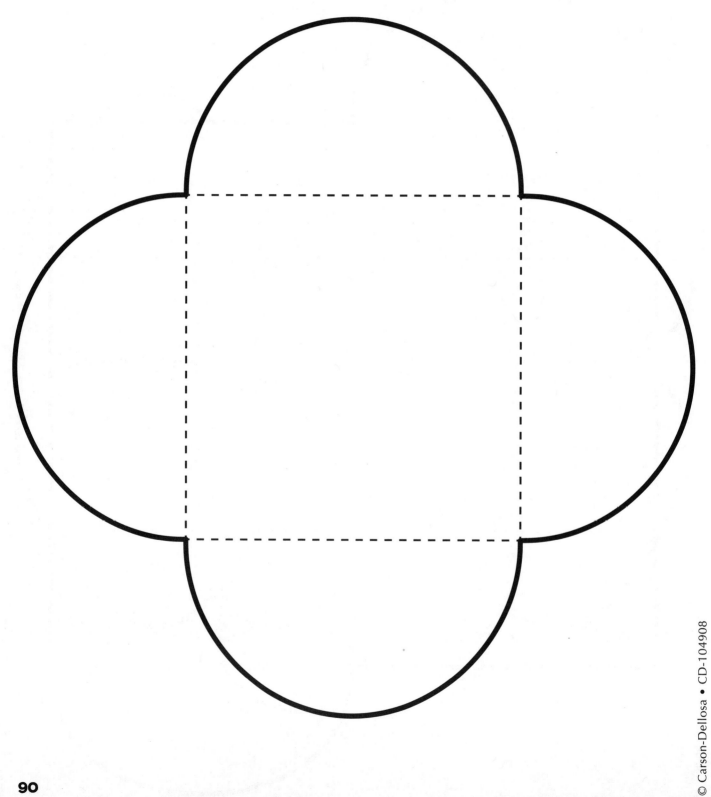

Six-Flap Petal Fold

Cut out the shape on the solid lines. Then, fold the flaps toward the center and back out. Apply glue to the back of the center panel to attach it to a notebook page.

Accordion Folds

Cut out the accordion pieces on the solid lines. Fold on the dashed lines, alternating the fold direction. Apply glue to the back of the last section to attach it to a notebook page.

You may modify the accordion books to have more or fewer pages by cutting off extra pages or by having students glue the first and last panels of two accordion books together.

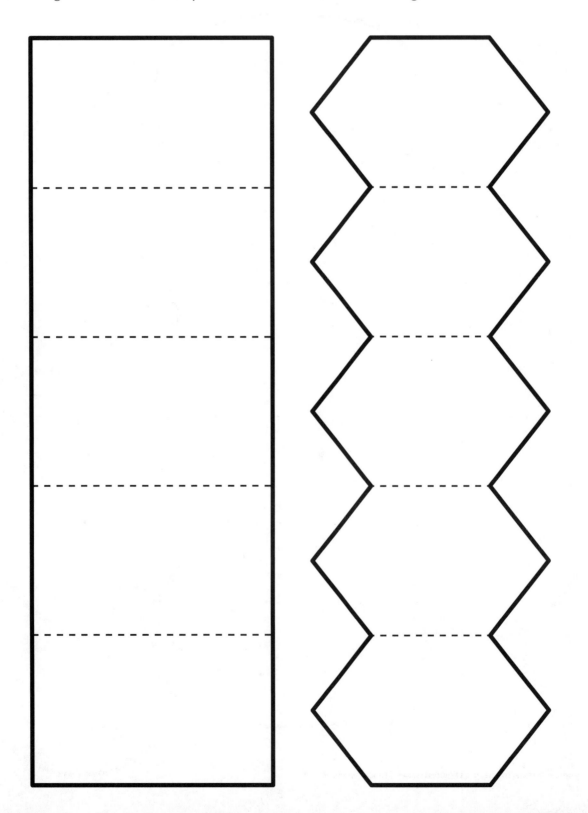

Accordion Folds

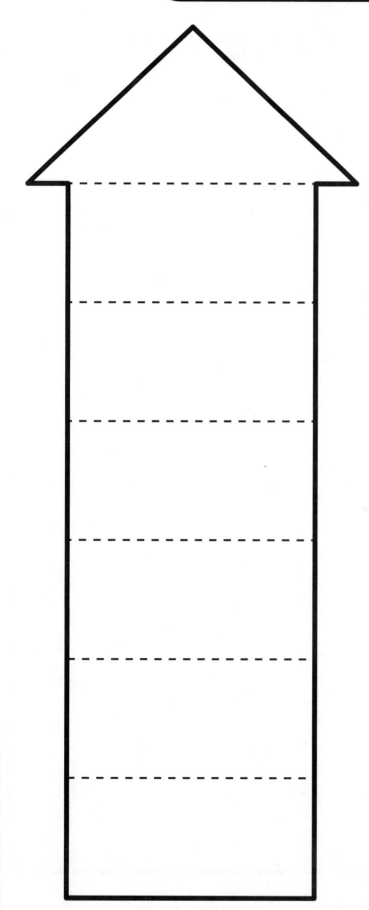

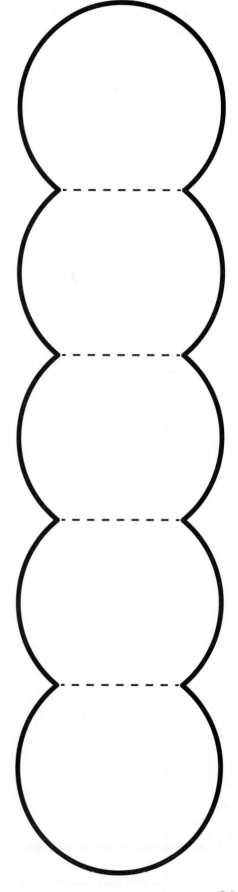

Clamshell Fold

Cut out the clamshell fold on the solid lines. Fold and unfold the piece on the three dashed lines. With the piece oriented so that the folds form an X with a horizontal line through it, pull the left and right sides together at the fold line. Then, keeping the sides touching, bring the top edge down to meet the bottom edge. You should be left with a triangular shape that unfolds into a square. Apply glue to the back of the triangle to attach the clamshell to a notebook page.

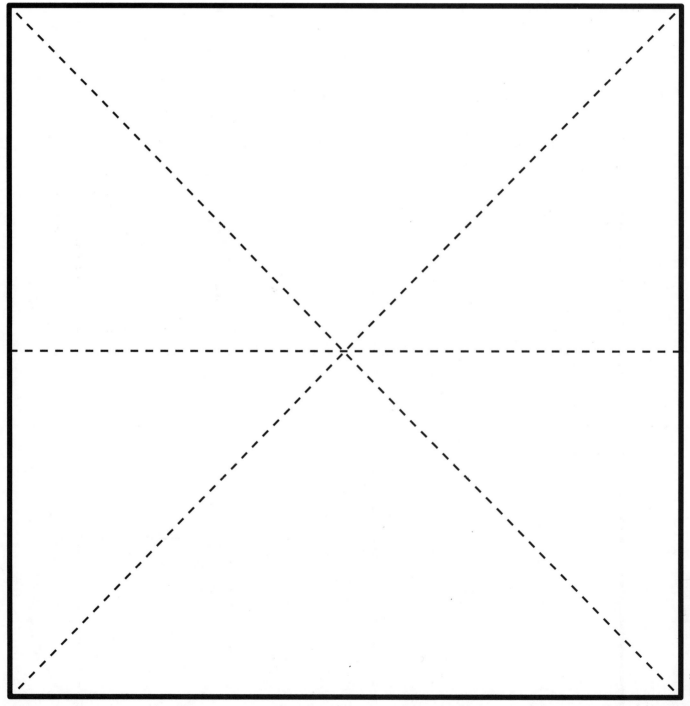

Puzzle Pieces

Cut out each puzzle along the solid lines to create a three- or four-piece puzzle. Apply glue to the back of each puzzle piece to attach it to a notebook page. Alternately, apply glue only to one edge of each piece to create flaps.

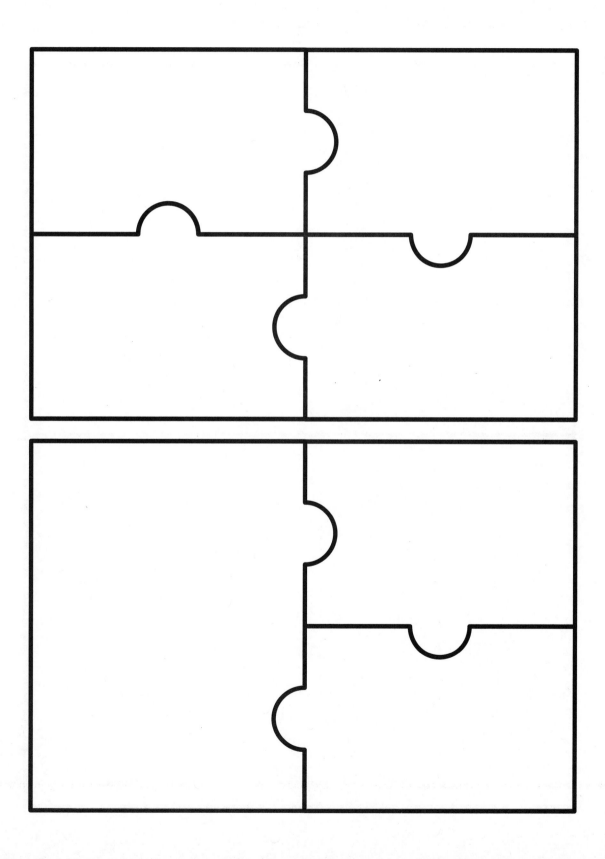

Flip Book

Cut out the two rectangular pieces on the solid lines. Fold each rectangle on the dashed lines. Fold the piece with the gray glue section so that it is inside the fold. Apply glue to the gray glue section and place the other folded rectangle on top so that the folds are nested and create a book with four cascading flaps. Make sure that the inside pages are facing up so that the edges of both pages are visible. Apply glue to the back of the book to attach it to a notebook page.

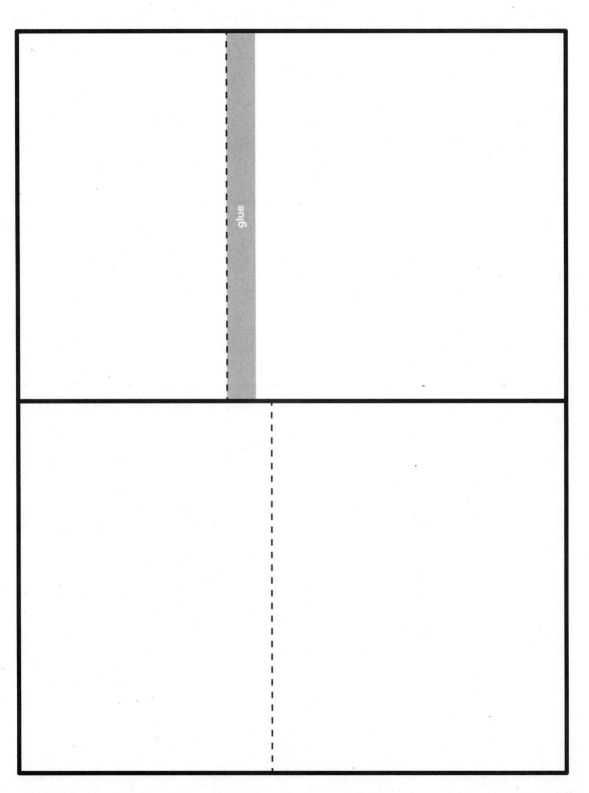

glue